CONTEMPORARY
CHINA

CONTEMPORARY CHINA'S DIPLOMACY

By Zhang Qingmin

 China Intercontinental Press

图书在版编目（CIP）数据

当代中国外交 : 英文 / 张清敏著 ; 张清敏译 . -- 北京 : 五洲传播出版社 , 2014.6（当代中国系列 / 武力主编）

ISBN 978-7-5085-2793-2

Ⅰ . ①当… Ⅱ . ①张… Ⅲ . ①外交－中国－现代－英文 Ⅳ . ① D82

中国版本图书馆 CIP 数据核字 (2014) 第 124450 号

当代中国系列丛书

主　　编：武　力
出 版 人：荆孝敏
统　　筹：付　平

当代中国外交

著　　者：张清敏
译　　者：张清敏
责 任 编 辑：王　峰
图 片 提 供：中新社　CFP　东方 IC
装 帧 设 计：丰饶文化传播有限责任公司
出 版 发 行：五洲传播出版社
地　　址：北京市海淀区北三环中路 31 号生产力大楼 B 座 7 层
邮　　编：100088
电　　话：010-82005927，82007837
网　　址：www.cicc.org.cn
承 印 者：中煤涿州制图印刷厂北京分厂
版　　次：2014 年 6 月第 1 版第 1 次印刷
开　　本：787×1092mm 1/16
印　　张：13.75
字　　数：180 千字
定　　价：108.00 元

Contents

Preface

As its economy continues to grow, China is already standing under the world's limelight. From the way it is looked at, we see both appreciation and suspicion, both recognition and criticism, and both welcome and questioning. But above all, expectation is the mainstream views—expectation for a fast-growing China to undertake its due responsibilities and make greater contribution to world peace and common development.

The development of China's diplomacy in the past decades tells the world that China's diplomacy has both the universal and international features of diplomacy but it has its own national features of Chinese culture. The experience of China's diplomacy is not only the treasure of China's diplomacy and the backing and base for its future but a contribution to international diplomatic theory and practice.

Diplomacy is "the conduct of adjustment and management of interstate relations." Ever since the emergence of nation state diplomacy has played a positive and significant role in coordinating interstate relations, maintaining world peace and promoting progress of human being. Inter-state connections are becoming ever more intimated in today's world of globalization, diplomacy is the most dynamic and most influence international politics.

Diplomacy is the bond that connects China and the world. The goal of China's diplomacy is to maintain good relations between China and the outside world: for China to engage in international affairs, to be integrated into the world system and enhance world's understanding of China. The evolution of New China's diplomacy since its founding demonstrates the situation of China's

On October 8, 2013, Cui Tiankai, ambassador of China to the United States, made a speech in the School of Advanced International Studies, Johns Hopkins University. During the speech, he raised the Chinese characters "Peace" he hand written personally and clarified that this was the fundamental philosophy of foreign affairs of China.

relations with the world. China's influence on the world and the world's influence on China are both unprecedented. The world's opportunities are also China's opportunities; and China's opportunities will also become the opportunities for the world. China's diplomacy has played key role during this process and at the same time China's diplomacy got improved and became matured.

Diplomacy is "the peaceful exercise of sovereignty by state." Diplomacy is one of the means for state to implement its foreign policy, but not the only means. Aggravated national power is the foundation and backing for diplomacy but diplomacy is not the show of muscle but "the application of intelligence and tact to the conduct of relations between the governments of independent states." The essential requirements for and the first characteristics of diplomacy are its very nature of peace.

Independence and peace-loving are the two fundamental features of China's diplomacy and the cornerstone of China's foreign policy. To maintain world peace and promote common progress are the very goals of China's diplomacy. China holds for peaceful settlement of international conflict and hot issues, opposes to resort to the use of force or the threat of force, and opposes to regime changes from outside. China insists on developing comprehensive friendly relations with all countries on the basis of Five Principles of Peaceful Co-existence.

"Diplomacy is the process of implementing foreign policy." The goal of a country's foreign policy is to further its national interest, so is the main goal and function of diplomacy which is the means to implement foreign policy. China's diplomacy is firm in upholding its core interests which include state sovereignty, national security, territorial integrity and national reunification, China's political system established by the Constitution and overall social stability, and the basic safeguards for ensuring sustainable economic and social development. While upholding its own national interest and the legitimate rights and interests of its citizens and corporations, China gives full respect to the rights of other countries in upholding their legitimate right in its diplomacy. While furthering its goal of national development, its also takes into consideration the lawful concern and interests, forging a close net of common interest forming countries community of common destiny with more intertwined interests.

Diplomacy is an important part of national grand strategy. As the international and domestic environment and national grand strategy changed, China's diplomatic strategies also changed. In the rather long period of time after the founding of New China, the main task of China's diplomacy was to safeguard China's sovereignty and territorial integrity. As the focus of China's domestic work switched to economic construction, the task of China's diplomacy changed to that of serving and promoting the central task of development to create a sound external environment for completing the building of a moderately prosperous society. The task of China's diplomacy today is to sever and promote the "two centenary goals (a moderately prosperous society by 2020 and a modern socialist country by 2049)" and realizing the great rejuvenation of the Chinese nation.

"Diplomacy is the exercise of sovereignty of independent states through official action." "Diplomacy is no small matter, the power belong to the Central government." The very nature of diplomatic work called for stronger top-level planning and medium- to long-term strategic planning. In a socialist country where the The Communist Party of China (CPC) is the leading force, the CPC Central Committee, its Political Bureau and its Standing Committee are the institutes of foreign policy making. To ensure the Central Committee's centralized and united leadership on diplomacy and foreign affairs and the smooth implementation of these decision, institution-building are being improved, relevant systems and mechanisms are being sorted out, and the administration of foreign related issues are further strengthened and standardized.

Diplomacy has strong characteristics of its time. The forms, means, and tools of diplomacy are not only constrained by global balance of power, but shaped by international customs and norms. The process that China's diplomacy matures is one during which China adapts to, accepts, and contributes to these norms. The expansion of diplomatic agendas, the increase of diplomatic stake-holders, diversification of communication channels and other new developments once again are promoting the transformation in diplomacy. In conform to the changes in international situation and meet the demand of the time, China takes steps to promote public diplomacy as well as people-to-people and cultural exchanges. It conducts friendly exchanges with political parties and organizations of other countries and encourages people's congresses, national and local committees of the Chinese People's Political Consultative Conference (CPPCC), local governments and people's organizations to increase overseas exchanges so as to consolidate the social foundation for enhancing China's relations with other countries.

Diplomacy not only has world and international national features, but it has more national and state features. The features of China's diplomacy originate from the rich and profound China's traditional culture, emphasizing the ideas of non-offense and good-neighborliness and peace being of paramount importance. These features are founded on China's national situation, insisting on peaceful development. These features rooted in the socialist ideas that China follows combining China's interest and the interest of peoples of the world in diplomacy and international affairs. These features are demonstrated in the practice of China's diplomacy and will continue to drive and guide China's diplomacy in the future.

Diplomacy is the extension of domestic politics. Domestic politics determines the nature a country's foreign policy and its diplomacy. The development of globalization has blurred the border between domestic and international politics and the interaction between the two is becoming ever broader and deeper. Starting from the point of coordinating the overall situation home and abroad, the CPC Central Committee attaches great importance to the coordination of China's domestic and international agenda. It emphasizes for a holistic management of foreign affairs. It calls for balanced considerations, overall planning, unified command and coordinated implementation. It calls for the central and local governments, non-governmental organizations and all foreign policy-related agencies to work together to form synergy, with each performing their respective functions.

China and the world are fully integrated through benign interaction. China cannot develop without the world and world peace also needs China's cooperation and contribution. This book tries to offer an overall picture in brief of the evolution and changes of China diplomacy during this interaction process, illustrates the development and driving forces of China's relations with and policies toward major countries and areas of the world, and elaborates China's position and policy on important international issues. By doing so it tries to present the remarkable features of China's diplomacy.

Aims of China's Diplomacy

Unswervingly adhering to the road of peaceful development is the sincere desire and unshakable choice of the Chinese people.

Constructing a harmonious world of sustained peace and common prosperity is the fundamental aspiration and unremitting goal of China's diplomacy.

Giving birth to one of the four ancient great civilizations, China has donated marvelous contributions to the world. In developing its relations with peripheral nations and countries in its long history, China has formed a China-centered and moral-based harmonious system, which is referred to as "Chinese-Barbarian Order" or "Tribute System."

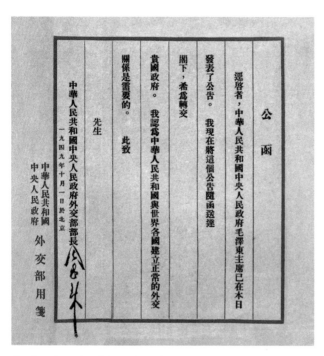

On October 1, 1949, Zhou Enlai, then Minister of Foreign Affairs, sent a letter of announcement of the People's Republic of China to the governments of various countries to express the willingness of New China on establishing normal diplomatic relations with them.

The Western powers forced open China's door with their warships and cannons in the 19th century. In the 100 years after the first Opium War in the 1840s, China, suffering from one invasion after another, was declined to a semi-colonial and semi-feudal country. Eliminating war and achieving peace, and establishing an independent, rich country where its people could live a happy life have become the assiduous goals for which the Chinese people have struggled in recent history.

Led by the The Communist Party of China (CPC), the Chinese people of different ethnic groups, after a long period of difficult and tortuous struggle, overthrew the rule of imperialism, feudalism and bureaucratic capitalism, succeeded in new democratic revolution, and founded the PRC in 1949. China's diplomacy opened a new chapter from then on.

The new Chinese government has held high the banner of peace, development, and cooperation, and insisted on the peaceful foreign policy of independence. The *Common Program* adopted by the Chinese People's Political Consultative Conference on September 30, 1949 says, "The foreign policy principle of the People's Republic of China is protection of the independence, freedom, and integrity of the territorial and sovereignty of the country, upholding lasting international peace and the friendly cooperation between peoples of all countries, and opposition to the imperialist policy of aggression and war."

Reaffirming the above provision, the first Constitution of New China enacted in 1954 announces to the world: "On international affairs, our unswerving principle is to work for the holy goal of world peace and human progress." In the past half century, China has consistently been a proponent of peaceful means, and has remained in strong opposition to using or threatening to use military force either in handling its relations with big powers, or in the settlement of issues with its neighbors that

In May 1987, Javier Perez de Cuellar, secretary-general of the United Nations, presented a glided copper dove of peace to Comrade Deng Xiaoping, state leader of China, expressing the appreciation and recognition of the United Nations to China as an important force safeguarding the world peace and stability.

are left over from history, or in the settlement of international disputes or regional hot issues that are not directly related to China's interests.

Since its reform and opening-up in 1978, China has, following the changes in the international community, grasped peace and development as the two major themes of the present era; persisted on economic construction as the core; emphasized that diplomacy was to create a long lasting peaceful international and peripheral environment for domestic economic constructions; held high the banner of peace; stabled its relations with big powers; cemented friendly cooperation with its neighboring countries; consolidated traditional friendship with other developing countries; actively participated in multilateral diplomacy; advocated for a new international political and economic order on the basis of the five principles of peaceful co-existence.

Facing the new international environment, China has continued to develop its proposal for international political and economic order, promoted the development of multi-polarization, and advocated the democratization of international relations and diversification of economic development modes. China has successively put forward the new concept of security, the new concept of civilization and development, and the guideline of building a good neighborly relationship and partnership with its neighbors. China also has tried its utmost to co-exist peacefully and share prosperity with other countries as it seeks to develop and strengthen itself.

In his speech to the Asia-Africa Summit held in Jakarta in April 2005, Chinese President Hu Jintao proposed that Asian and African countries should work together to construct a harmonious world featuring friendly co-existence among different civilizations, conduct dialogue on an equal footing, and strengthen development and prosperity. In his speech to the United Nations in September the same

On September 15, 2005, H. E. Hu Jintao, president of China, made an important speech *Build Towards a Harmonious World of Lasting Peace and Common Prosperity* at the United Nations Summit to commemorate the 60th anniversary of the founding of the United Nations.

year, he further elaborated the ideas of "building a harmonious world of sustained peace and common prosperity," revealing the new perspective on world affairs with Chinese characteristics.

The idea of building a harmonious world of sustained peace and common prosperity is inherited from earlier Chinese diplomatic thoughts and is a distillation of those thoughts. It emphasizes coordination of interests of different parties and resolving conflicts that may exist among them, seeking win-win results to further their utmost interests, and to gain win-win goals through peaceful and cooperative means, given that diversity, conflicts of interest, and the co-existence of different civilizations are the reality of the world. The idea of "building a harmonious world" is also the demonstration of the peace-loving elements in Chinese traditional culture in managing China's relations with other countries in ancient times, which is built upon good-neighborliness. The concept of a harmonious world is consistent with the spirit of the *UN Charter* and the domestic policies of China, embodies the unity of China's peaceful development and the world's stability and prosperity, and the unity of the fundamental interests of both the Chinese people and people throughout the world.

Building a harmonious world of sustained peace and common prosperity is the lofty goal of China on the road of peaceful development. China holds that a harmonious world should be democratic, friendly, fair, and tolerant. To reach this goal, China advocates the following principles:

1. Upholding democracy and equality to achieve coordination and cooperation. All countries should, on the basis of the *UN Charter* and the Five Principles of Peaceful Coexistence, promote democracy in international relations through dialogue, communication and cooperation. The internal affairs of a country should be decided by its people. International affairs should be discussed and solved by all countries on an equal footing. Developing countries ought to enjoy the equal right to participate in and make decisions on international affairs. All countries should respect each other and treat each other equally. No country is entitled to impose its own will upon others, or maintain its security and development at the price of the interests of others. When dealing with international relations, it is necessary to persist in proceeding from the common interests of all the people throughout the world, make efforts to expand common interests, enhance understanding through communication, strengthen cooperation through understanding, and create a win-win situation through cooperation.

On April 7, 2013, H.E. Xi Jinping, president of China, delivered a keynote speech *Working Together Toward a Better Future for Asia and the World at* Boao Forum for Asia 2013 Annual Conference.

2. Upholding harmony and mutual trust to realize common security. All countries should join hands to respond to threats against world security. We should abandon the Cold War mentality, and cultivate a new security concept featuring mutual trust, mutual benefit, equality and coordination. We should build a fair and effective collective security mechanism aimed at jointly preventing conflict and war, and cooperate to eliminate or reduce as much as possible threats from non-traditional security problems such as terrorist activities, financial crises and natural disasters, so as to safeguard world peace, security and stability. We should persist in settling international disputes and conflicts peacefully through consultations and negotiations on the basis of equality, and work together to oppose acts of encroachment on the sovereignty of other countries, interference in the internal affairs of

other countries, and willful use or threat of use of military force. We should step up cooperation in a resolute fight against terrorism, stamp out both the symptoms and root causes of the problem of terrorism, with special emphasis on eliminating the root cause of the menace. We should achieve effective disarmament and arms control in a fair, rational, comprehensive and balanced fashion, prevent the proliferation of weapons of mass destruction, vigorously promote the international nuclear disarmament process, and maintain global strategic stability.

3. Upholding fairness and mutual benefit to achieve common development. In the process of economic globalization, we should stick to the principle of fairness, achieve balanced and orderly development, and benefit all countries, developing countries in particular, instead of further widening of the gap between South and North. We should propel economic globalization towards the direction of common prosperity. The developed countries should shoulder a greater responsibility for a universal, coordinated and balanced development of the world, while the developing countries should make full use of their own advantages to achieve development. We should actively further trade and investment liberalization and facilitation, remove all kinds of trade barriers, increase market access, and ease restrictions on technology export, so as to establish an international multilateral trading system that is public, fair, rational, transparent, open and nondiscriminatory, and construct a good trading environment conducive to orderly global economic development. We should further improve the international financial system to create a stable and highly efficient financial environment. We should step up worldwide dialogue and cooperation in the field of energy, and jointly maintain energy security and energy market stability. We should actively promote and guarantee human rights to ensure that everyone enjoys equal opportunities and the right to pursue overall

development. We should make innovations in development, promote the harmonious development of man and nature, and take the road of sustainable development.

4. Upholding tolerance and creating an open society to achieve dialogue among civilizations. Diversity of civilizations is a basic feature of human society, and an important driving force for the progress of mankind. All countries should respect other country's right to independently choose their own social systems and paths of development, learn from one another and draw on the strong points of others to make up for their own weak points, thus achieving rejuvenation and development in line with their own national conditions. Dialogues and exchanges among civilizations should be encouraged, doing away with misgivings and estrangement between civilizations. We should develop together by seeking common ground while putting aside differences, so as to make mankind more harmonious and the world more colorful. We should endeavor to preserve the diversity of civilizations and development patterns, and jointly build a harmonious world where all civilizations coexist and accommodate one another.

The world today is facing unprecedented opportunities and challenges. However the situation changes, China is determined to hold high the banner of peace, development, and cooperation, persist in taking the road of peaceful development, pursue the opening-up strategy of mutual benefit with all as winners, and promote the building of a harmonious world with enduring peace and common prosperity. This is a solemn commitment of the Chinese government!

Since the formation of the new Chinese Government in 2013, the Secretary General of the CPC Central Committee Xi Jinping put forward the notion of "Chinese dream" and has elaborated the meaning of "Chinese dream" on important diplomatic occasions. He said that the Chinese Dream is a dream for peace, development, cooperation and mutual benefit for all, a dream that connects China rejuvenation with world progress, and an important link between China and the world.

Xi proposes that China should uphold fairness and justice and adhere to the principle of mutual benefits and common development in its diplomacy. He also underscores that China should think others more in its relations with neighboring and other developing countries and think about justice before interest and sacrifice the latter for the former if necessary. He also emphasizes that China should make progress in its development in a harmonized environment where China enjoys mutual beneficial relations and attaining common progress with other countries of the world.

Principles of China's Diplomacy

Diplomacy is the official exercise of sovereignty externally by independent state and an important means for a country to defend its interests and implement its foreign policy. Diplomatic independence is impossible without the independence of national sovereignty.

Ever since its founding, New China has achieved and consolidated its national and diplomatic independence, maintained national security and territorial integrity, and has gained China's equal status and dignity on the international stage. China cherishes its hard-won independence and respects the independence of other countries, and makes it the fundamental principle of its foreign policy.

The Development of Independent Foreign Policy

Seeking national independence has been the consistent goal of the Chinese people in recent history.

The history of China's external relations in the 100 years before the founding of the PRC in 1949 was one subjected to endless bullying and humiliation, and old China's diplomacy was one of humiliation. Since the first Opium War in 1940, the imperialist powers forced upon the late Qing government a series of unequal treaties, by which they seized many prerogatives in China, including leaseholds, spheres of influence, open ports, extraterritorialities, and

On October 1, 1949, the People's Republic of China was founded and Mao Zedong read out the announcement of the central government on Tiananmen Gate Tower.

unilateral most-favored nation status, among others. Numerous Chinese people with high ideals in recent history have waged tireless and arduous struggles for China's national independence and liberation, but all failed to change China's fate. By the time the PRC was founded, the west imperialists still enjoyed such privileges in China as stationing troops, carrying on free trade, navigating inland, maintaining jurisdiction and customs administrations, and setting tariffs.

On October 1, 1949, the People's Republic of China was founded. Chinese people finally stood up with their national independence and liberation! Thereafter the main diplomatic task of New China has become safeguarding national independence, territorial integrity, and sovereignty.

It was imperative to thoroughly do away with the prerogatives imperialists enjoyed in China, and have a clear break with the "heritage" of Old China's diplomacy of humiliation in order to achieve independence. The new Chinese government adopted and carried out three major foreign policies upon its founding, namely "cleaning up the house before entertaining guests," "starting anew," and "leaning to one side."

To implement the policy of "cleaning up the house before entertaining guests," new laws were promulgated to gradually clear up the political, economic and cultural prerogatives enjoyed by the imperialists that were left over from Old China. The implementation of this policy changed the situation that China had to depend upon other countries, making it an independent country in political, economic, and cultural realms.

To carry out the policy of "starting anew," it is imperative to break up the Old China's diplomacy of humiliation, and renounce the diplomatic relations the Old Chinese government had established with foreign countries, and start New China's diplomatic relations with foreign countries on the basis of equality between independent states. As for those who did not want to recognize or develop relations with the new Chinese government on an equal footing, China would not recognize the diplomatic missions accredited to old China as diplomatic envoys. As for the treaties or agreements made between the old Chinese government with foreign countries, the new Chinese government, after a review, would recognize, abrogate, revise, or re-negotiate according to their respective contents.

The principle of establishing diplomatic relations through negotiation

"Starting anew" requires the new Chinese government insist on the procedure of establishing diplomatic relations with other countries through negotiation. Article 56 of the *Common Program* passed by CPPCC in 1949, which functioned as provincial Constitution, provides, "The Central People's Government of the People's Republic of China may, on the basis of equality, mutual benefit and mutual respect for territorial and sovereignty, negotiate with foreign government which have served relations with the Kuomintang reactionary clique and which take a friendly attitude towards the People's Republic of China, and may establish diplomatic relations with them." This is known as the principle of "establishing diplomatic relations through negotiation."

This principle takes into consideration the fact the former Nationalist Government has fled to Taiwan and regards severing diplomatic ties with the old nationalist government in Taiwan as a precondition and testimony if the country has adopted a friendly attitude toward New China and abides by the principle of equality, mutual benefit and mutual respect for each other's territory integrity and sovereignty. This principle is a contribution to the international practice on establishing diplomatic ties and has remained effective in China's diplomacy till today.

By pursuing the policy of "leaning to one side," New China took its stand in the socialist camps headed by the Soviet Union according to the different policies and attitudes of United States and the Soviet Union toward New China against the backdrop of the Cold War confrontation between the East and the West. Upon the founding of the PRC, the *Common Program* adopted by the Chinese People's Political Consultative Conference clearly states, "The People's Republic of China shall unite with all peace-loving and freedom-loving countries and peoples throughout the world, first of all, with the U.S.S.R., all peoples' democracies and all oppressed nations. It shall take its stand in the camp of international peace and democracy, to oppose imperialist aggression, and to defend lasting world peace."

To carry out the policy of "leaning to one side," Chairman Mao Zedong paid a visit to the Soviet Union upon the founding of New China. The two sides signed in February 1950 *Sino-Soviet Treaty of Friendship, Alliance and Mutual Assistance*, in which the two parties undertake to cement Sino-Soviet friendly cooperation and jointly prevent a repetition of imperialist aggression. The Sino-Soviet treaty provided China with a reliable ally and a guarantee for its security.

On October 2, 1949, the Soviet Union became the first country establishing the diplomatic ties with New China.

Opposing the threats from superpowers and safeguarding national security was the main task for maintaining New China's independence in the early days after its founding. After the outbreak of the Korean War in June 1950, American President Harry Truman issued a declaration ordering U.S. forces to intervene directly in the Korean War and the American seventh fleet to deploy in the Taiwan Straits. He also ordered to increase the American military presence in the Philippines and the American military assistance to French troops in Indochina. Truman's declaration connected the Korean Peninsula, Taiwan Straits, and Southeast Asia with the same target at the newly-founded China. While intervening in the Korean War, U.S. military aircraft intruded into China's airspace over Northeast China and bombed and strafed Chinese villages along the Sino-Korean border. At the same time, the U.S. manipulated the UN, while the PRC's legitimate seat in the UN was deprived, passed resolutions to impose sanctions against China. The U.S. navy forced interrogations and examinations

In June 1950, Sweden became the first western country establishing the diplomatic relations with China.

on Chinese commercial ships on the high seas, encroaching on the Chinese rights of free voyage and causing great damage and losses to Chinese people's lives and property.

China was forced to get involved in the Korean War, and in the end, won the war to resist U.S. aggression and aid Korea, brought peace to the Korean Peninsula, meeting the goal of defending the country and protecting People's home, raised China's international status, and greatly enhanced China's independence, sovereignty, and security. In Indochina, China supported the struggles of the Indochinese people for their national independence, actively participated in the Geneva conference, which restored peace to Indochina and eliminated the U.S. threat toward China from the south. Thereafter, the core and key issue in China's relations with the U.S. shifted to the opposition of the U.S. infringement upon the Chinese territory of Taiwan, and the opposition of U.S. interference in China's internal affairs. These have remained as two of China's major foreign policy tasks until today.

Independence has been New China's fundamental diplomatic principle. It has been the most important feature that makes New China's diplomacy remarkably different from that of Old China and has penetrated to every aspect of New China's diplomacy. During the 1950s when the "leaning to one side" policy was China's foreign policy strategy, Mao Zedong, Zhou Enlai and other Chinese leaders repeatedly exhorted that we should not have the desire to depend upon the Soviet Union and we should not follow the Soviets experiences blindly. They said that China should think with its own brains and walk on its own feet, that "although strategically we are allies, tactically we should not relinquish our right of criticism." Due to the differences in their international positions, China and the Soviet Union began to have different views on the international structure as well as diplomatic strategies, especially their strategies toward the U.S., from the late 1950s. The Soviet Union tried to bring China into its track of "Soviet-U.S. cooperation for world domination." Under great pressure, Mao Zedong and other

Chinese leaders declined the suggestions from the Soviets' side, which would have undermined China's sovereignty and diplomatic independence, and instead upheld China's independence in its relations with other socialist countries.

The international situation underwent major changes in late 1960s. The U.S. was greatly impaired as it was bogged down in the quagmire of the Vietnam War, while the Soviet Union seized the opportunity and started expansionism with its power increased. After U.S. President Richard Nixon took office, he put forward the Nixon Doctrine with an attempt to reduce the U.S. presence in the Asian Pacific areas and the world as a whole. At the same time, the Soviet leader put forward the Brezhnev Doctrine, the core of which was that the Soviet Union was entitled to interfere in the internal affairs of other Socialist countries. The two "doctrines" symbolized the decrease of the U.S. threat and the increase of the Soviet threat toward China. Realizing the Soviet Union had become the major threat to Chinese security and world peace, China started to improve its relations with the U.S.

From April to July, 1954, Zhou Enlai, premier and Minister of Foreign Affairs, headed a delegation to attend Geneva Conference which was convened to address outstanding issues of North Korea and restore peace in Indo-China. The picture is the group photo of members of the delegation.

As the Soviet threat toward China increased, China pursued a foreign policy strategy of opposing the two superpowers of the U.S. and the Soviet Union with a focus on opposing the Soviet hegemonism in the 1970s. In his meeting with foreign guests in 1973, Mao Zedong proposed, "The U.S., Japan, and China, connected with Pakistan, Iran, Turkey, the Arab World, and Europe, should all get united; one big area of the Third World should get united" to oppose to the Soviet threat.

From the late 1970s to the early 1980s, the Soviets' expansionism encountered difficulties after its invasion against Afghanistan, while the U.S. started to roll back the Soviets. The international balance of power witnessed a new shift to a virtue of balance between the two superpowers. The likelihood of war diminished and the threat China faced declined, and it became possible for China to concentrate on domestic economic construction. After the Third Plenary Session of the 11th Central Committee in 1978, China made further emphasis on adhering to the principle of independence in its foreign relations as it made

In April 1971, Premier Zhou Enlai received the US table tennis delegation and the door to China-US diplomacy was thus opened. That was the famous Pingpong Diplomacy.

domestic policy adjustment. In his opening remarks at the 12th National Congress of the CPC in 1982, Deng Xiaoping reiterated, "China's affairs should be run according to China's specific conditions and by the Chinese people themselves. Independence and self-reliance have always been, and will always be, their basic stand. While the Chinese people value their friendship and cooperation with other countries and peoples, they value even more their hard-won independence and sovereign right. No foreign country should expect China to be its vassal or to accept anything that is damaging to China's own interests."

When a political incident happened in China in 1989, some western countries led by the U.S. made unwarranted charges against China, interfered in China's internal affairs, and even imposed sanctions on China. While meeting with foreign guests, Deng pointed out, "Sovereignty and national security should always be the priority. We are clearer than we were ever before," and "China will never allow any country to interfere in its internal affairs." The Chinese government retained a sober mind, persisted on the peaceful foreign policy of independence, and successfully broke those sanctions in the end, safeguarding national independence and sovereignty.

Facing the pressures from the West since the 1990s, China did not compromise or give in. Rather, China became more resolute in safeguarding its national sovereignty, national interests, and national dignity. In light of that, some countries advocated after the Cold War that "human rights are more important than sovereignty" and other theories that go against the purpose and principles of the *UN Charter* and infringe upon the principles of internal law and other international norms. China continued to adhere to the principle of independence, resolutely opposed to any country's interference in China's internal affairs for whatever excuse.

The world has undergone tremendous changes and adjustments since the end of the Cold War and the traditional concept of security has changed as well. In addition to territorial integrity and sovereignty non-interference, which remain

In November 2012, the 18th National Congress of the CPC was convened in Beijing. The report of the 18th National Congress pointed out that China will strive to uphold world peace and promote common development, and unswervingly follow the path of peaceful development and firmly pursue an independent foreign policy of peace.

the major security issues, non-traditional security issues—such as economic security, cultural security, information security, ecological security, and cross-border crimes, proliferation of nuclear technology, ethnic strife, drug trafficking, terrorism, and trans-border migrations—have become more and more salient. As the Political Report to the 18th National Congress the CPC states: China commits that it will continue to hold high the banner of peace, development, cooperation and mutual benefit and strive to uphold world peace and promote common development and that it will unswervingly follow the path of peaceful development and firmly pursue an independent foreign policy of peace. China is firm in its resolve to uphold China's sovereignty, security and development interests, will never yield to any outside pressure, and will work to uphold fairness and justice.

The Contents of Independent Foreign Policy

Ever since its founding, the PRC's diplomatic strategies and specific foreign policies have undergone changes and adjustments with the changes in the international situation, but it has been basically characterized by the maintenance of independence in different times. Having run through its history, the principles of independence have developed, revealing the diplomatic features with Chinese characteristic. As a fundamental principle of Chinese foreign policy, independent foreign policy includes the following major aspects:

China is a unified, multi-national country. Realizing national unity and maintaining national territorial integrity is a premise for independence and a notable manifestation of independent foreign policy. China can never tolerate an encroachment upon its national unity, territorial integrity, and national dignity. Under the complex domestic and international environment, opposing the threat to national unity and security from "Taiwan independence," "East Turkistan Islamic Movement," "Tibet Independence" and other secessionist forces is one premise and fundamental task for China's independent foreign policy.

Sovereignty is the fundamental attribute and symbol of nation-states. China holds that sovereign countries have the right to choose their own social system, independently determine their domestic and foreign policy, and choose their own road of national development completely by themselves without external inference. On international affairs, China values the rights of every people to choose their own roads of development by themselves, does not interfere in the international affairs of other countries, and does not impose our will on others, nor does China permit any other countries to interfere in China's internal affairs.

In April 1974, Deng Xiaoping headed the Chinese delegation to attend the 6th Special Session of the General Assembly of the United Nations and expounded the principles of China on the foreign relations.

By upholding independence, China advocates the democratization of international affairs. Countries, big or small, strong or weak, rich or poor, are all equal members of the international community. They should enjoy the same and equal rights and shoulder the same and equal obligation on issues that concern world peace and the development of human beings as a whole. On international affairs, China holds that all countries should uphold the purposes and principles of the United Nations Charter, and observe international law and other universally recognized norms of international relations. Politically, all countries should respect each other and conduct consultations on an equal footing in a common endeavor to promote democracy in international relations. Economically, they should cooperate with each other, draw on each other's strengths, and work together to advance economic globalization in the direction of balanced development, shared benefits and win-win progress. Culturally, they should learn from each other in the spirit of seeking common ground while shelving differences, respecting the diversity of the world, and making joint efforts to advance human civilization. On environmental issues, they should assist and cooperate with each other in conservation efforts to take good care of the Earth, the only home of human beings.

By holding independence, China supports any activities that are conducive to maintaining world strategic balance and stability. China holds that countries should enhance mutual understanding and trust, and endeavor to solve international disputes and conflicts through peaceful means. China advocates the new concept of security of mutual trust and mutual benefit, and equality and cooperation to maintain regional and global security through cooperation of mutual benefits. China advocates solving international contradictions through consultation. China proposes seeking stability through cooperation and meeting the common challenges facing us through enhancing multilateral security cooperation. China opposes the use and threat of the use of force, any foreign attempt to subvert the legitimate government of any other countries, as well as the policies of war, aggression, expansion, and arms race.

In upholding independence, China does not enter into any alliances with any big powers or power blocks, or form military blocks, or engage in arms race or military expansion. China pursues a national defense policy that is defensive in nature. China does not seek spheres of influence; neither does China support one country opposing another. China opposes hegemonism and commits that it will never seek hegemony, will never engage in expansionism, or pose a military threat to any other country.

In upholding independence, China develops friendly cooperation of mutual benefit with all countries according to the five principles of peaceful co-existence. China does not decide its relations with other countries according to any ideological standards or social systems. China is "prepared to maintain contacts and make friends with everyone." China is not influenced or controlled by any specific issue at any specific time. Rather it is determined to develop omni-directional relations with all countries in light of the overall situation of maintaining world peace and promoting economic development.

In upholding independence, China never yields to any external pressure. Rather it decides its position and policy on international issues according to the interests of the people of China and the world at large, to the merits of the issues themselves, to whether it is conducive to maintaining world peace and stability, to whether it can promote cooperation among countries, promote the prosperity of the world economy, culture, and human progress.

Opposing Splitting the Nation, Safeguarding National Unity and Territorial Integrity

One premise for diplomatic independence is to realize and maintain national unity and secure national territorial integrity. China's foreign policy of independence is first reflected in its consistent opposition to foreign interference in China's internal affairs, in its struggle for reunification of the two sides of the Taiwan Straits, and in its diplomatic practice to resume the exercise of sovereignty over Hong Kong and Macau.

Taiwan is an inalienable part of Chinese territory. After the war against China in 1895, Japan forced the Qing Government to sign the *Treaty of Shimonoseki* and occupied Taiwan thereafter. In December 1943, the governments of China, the U.S., and Great Britain issued the *Cairo Declaration*, which stipulated that Japan return all the territories that she has seized or occupied, including Northeast China, Taiwan, and Penghu to China. The *Potsdam Proclamation* signed by China, the U. S. and Great Britain on July 26, 1945, which was subsequently adhered to by the Soviet Union, reiterated that the terms of the *Cairo Declaration* shall be carried out. In August of the same year, Japan surrendered. The condition of the surrender was that Japan accepted the provisions in the declaration. On Oct. 25, the Chinese government recovered Taiwan, Penghu, and resumed sovereignty over Taiwan. Taiwan and Penghu had been put back under the jurisdiction of Chinese sovereignty not only de jure but de facto.

The government of the PRC was founded on Oct.1, 1949, replacing the government of the Republic of China (ROC) to become the sole legitimate government of all China and the only legitimate representative of China internationally. Some of the ruling Nationalist Party and the administrative officials of the old ROC government withdrew to and took refuge in Taiwan, creating a situation of separation on the two sides of the Taiwan Straits. The Taiwan issue is left over from China's Civil War. Striving for national reunification of Taiwan and the mainland is China's domestic affair. The Taiwan issue concerns China sovereignty and territorial integrity, and bears on the national sentiments of the 1.3 billion Chinese people. The Chinese Government has been in strong opposition to any foreign government's interference in China's internal affairs on the Taiwan issue.

Against the backdrop of East-West confrontation, the U.S. deployed its seventh fleet to the Taiwan Straits when the Korean War broke out in 1950, and signed a *Mutual Defense Treaty* with the Taiwan authorities in 1954, bringing China's Taiwan Province under the U.S. "protection." The U.S. policy infringed upon China's territory integrity and sovereignty, causing long-lasting tension in the Taiwan Straits area.

In October 1987, the Taiwan authorities made the decision to permit Taiwan compatriots to visit their relatives on the mainland and the Taiwan compatriots were very exciting after climbing the Great Wall.

The U.S. supported Taiwan authority to confront with the mainland and prevented the realization of China's national reunification. These are the best demonstrations of America's hostile policy toward China. Opposing America's interference in China's internal affairs on the Taiwan issue has been a long task in China's foreign relations. The Taiwan issue has been the focus of Sino-U.S. confrontation during the cold war, the core of the three Sino-U.S. communiques, and the key and most sensitive issue in Sino-US bilateral relations.

With the changes in international situation, Sino-U.S. relations started to relax in the late 1960s and early 1970s. In the Joint Communiqué issued in Shanghai during Nixon's visit to China in 1972, the U.S. stated, "The United States acknowledges that all Chinese on either side of the Taiwan Straits maintain that there is but one China and Taiwan is part of China. The United States does not challenge this position."

After the U.S. government accepted in December 1978 the three preconditions for establishing diplomatic relations raised by the Chinese government—that the U.S. sever its diplomatic ties with Taiwan, abrogate the *Mutual Defense Treaty* signed by the U.S. and the Taiwan authority, and withdraw its troops from Taiwan—China and the U.S. issued another joint communiqué on establishing diplomatic ties between the two countries. The communiqué provides, "The United States of America recognizes the Government of the People's Republic of China as the sole legal government of China. Within this context, the people of the United States will maintain cultural, commercial and other unofficial relations with the people of Taiwan... The government of the United States of America acknowledges the Chinese position that there is but one China and Taiwan is part of China."

China hoped that the relaxation of the bilateral relations and the final establishment of diplomatic ties between China and the U.S. could facilitate the reunification of the two sides of the Taiwan Straits. When Sino-U.S. diplomatic ties were established, the Chinese government, in order to promote world peace, made a change to the policy of "we must liberate Taiwan"—a policy China had promoted ever since its founding—and proposed the "one country, two systems" formula with an attempt to realize a peaceful reunification of the motherland.

However, the U.S. abandoned its policy not to interfere in China's internal affairs on the Taiwan issue after China and the U.S. established diplomatic ties. In March 1979, the U.S. Congress passed a so-called *Taiwan Relations Act*, which contains many provisions that contradict the Sino-US joint communiqué on establishing diplomatic ties and the principles of international law, including provisions that the U.S. will continue to sell weapons to Taiwan.

The U.S. sales of weapons to Taiwan caused the first crisis in Sino-U.S. relations after their normalizations. In order to solve the problems of American arms sales to Taiwan, the Chinese government and the U.S. government reached another agreement in August 1982 through negotiation, and the two sides issued the third joint communiqué in bilateral relations. The U.S. government states in the communiqué, "It does not seek to carry out a long-term policy of arms sales to Taiwan, that its arms sales to Taiwan will not exceed, either in qualitative or in quantitative terms, the level of those supplied in recent years since the establishment of diplomatic relations between the United States and China and that it intends gradually to reduce its sale of arms to Taiwan, leading, over a period of time, to a final resolution."

As Sino-US relations stabilized in the 1980s, the cross straits relations also relaxed. Non-official exchanges between the two sides of the Taiwan Straits started in 1987.

After the end of the Cold War, the Taiwan authorities changed its policy on reunification and gradually deviated from the "one China" stand to seek Taiwan "independence" in the name of so-called "expanding (Taiwan's) international space." The Taiwan authorities had made attempts to participate in the United Nations since 1993, and Lee Teng-hui, the leader of Taiwan authorities, even referred to the cross straits relations as "special state-to-state relations,"

In April 1993, Wang Daohan, president of the Association for Relations Across the Taiwan Straits, and Koo Chen-Fu, chairman of the Straits Exchange Foundation, held talks in Singapore. That was the first meeting of top leaders of the authorized non-governmental organizations across the Taiwan Straits.

making its Taiwan "independence" banner public. During this process, the U.S. government has time and again broken its commitments in the Aug, 17 Joint Communiqué, and upgraded its arms sales to Taiwan both in quantitative and qualitative terms. The U.S. decision to sell Taiwan 150 F-16s fighter planes in 1992, the package of advanced weapons sold to Taiwan in 2001 and 2008 by the U.S. government all violated its commitments on this issue, creating obstacles and new external blocks for the peaceful settlement of the Taiwan issue. The American policies have been strongly opposed to by the Chinese government and have resulted in several frictions and crises in the bilateral relations.

China not only opposes the U.S. sale of weapons to Taiwan but opposes any other countries selling weapons to Taiwan or entering into a military alliance with the Taiwan authorities. The Netherlands government, disregarding the Chinese government's opposition, insisted on selling weapons to Taiwan, leading to a downgrade of the bilateral relations in 1982. The French government's decision to sell weapons to Taiwan in 1992 also caused big twists and turns in Sino-French relations, which did not return to normal until after the French government reaffirmed its policy on this issue.

As the sole legitimate government of all China in the world, the PRC has a clear and consistent policy on Taiwan. There is but one China and Taiwan is an inalienable part of Chinese territory, and all countries that have diplomatic ties with China should respect the sovereignty and territorial integrity of China. China strongly opposes any country that has diplomatic relations with China from treating Taiwan as an "independent political entity," or establishing or developing official ties with Taiwan, or creating "dual recognition" in whatever form, or creating "two Chinas" or "one China, one Taiwan." This is a principle the PRC has insisted upon in developing its relations with other countries.

The Chinese government safeguards all the justified and lawful rights and interests of Taiwan compatriots abroad. On the basis of the one-China principle, the Chinese government has made arrangements for Taiwan's participation in some inter-governmental international organizations that accept regional memberships in an agreeable and acceptable way according to the nature, regulations and actual conditions of these international organizations. As a region of China, Taiwan has participated in the Asian Development Bank (ADB), the Asia-Pacific Economic Cooperation (APEC), and World Trade Organization respectively in the names of "Taipei, China," "Chinese Taipei," and "Chinese Taipei" as a separate Taiwan-Penghu-Jinmen-Mazu tariff zone.

Cross-Straits relations underwent a major change since 2008 and the three direct links (direct trade, transport and postal services communications) between the two sides have been established and Economic Cooperation Framework Agreement (ECFA) was signed and is now under implementation. Gradual integration of the two sides is undergoing through two-way interactions and cooperation. As to Taiwan's international status, Hu Jintao has pointed out that the Mainland understands Taiwan compatriots' desire to participate in

international activities. He said that the two sides should avoid internal struggle in foreign affairs and work for the interest of all Chinese. As for the prospect of Taiwan's non-official economic and cultural exchanges with foreign countries, the two sides can engage in further consultation in case of necessity. Hu said the mainland is willing to discuss with Taiwan and make reasonable arrangements for Taiwan's participation in international organizations, as long as this does not create a scenario of "two Chinas" or "China and Taiwan."

As for the Taiwan issue in Sino-U.S. relations, the Chinese Government believes that the issue—once a liability and negative factor in our relationship—will be turned into an asset and a positive factor, providing guarantee to the long-term, steady growth of China-US relations and opening prospect for all-round cooperation if the United States can go along with the prevailing trend of peaceful development of cross-Straits relations, and genuinely appreciate and respect China's efforts to oppose separation and achieve peaceful reunification.

On December 15, 2008, three direct links of trade, mail, and air and shipping services across the Taiwan Straits were officially launched. The picture is of the direct shipping freighter departing from Xiamen Port to Taiwan.

However the situation changes, the Chinese government is committed to the policy of "one country, two system" and peaceful reunification, and will make its utmost effort with the utmost sincerity to promote the peaceful development of cross-straits relations in an attempt to realize the prospect of peaceful reunification. But it has also made clear that it will never allow anyone to split Taiwan from the motherland in any form or in whatever name. The *Anti-Secession Law* passed by the Chinese National People's Congress in 2005 reaffirmed in legal terms the Chinese government's policy of peaceful reunification of the two sides of the Taiwan Straits, but it also provides that if "'Taiwan independence' secessionist forces should act under any name or by any means to cause the fact of Taiwan's secession from China, or that major incidents entailing Taiwan's secession from China should occur, or that possibilities for a peaceful reunification should be completely exhausted, the state shall employ non-peaceful means and other necessary measures to protect China's sovereignty and territorial integrity."

Resuming the Exercise of Sovereignty over Hong Kong and Macau in Accordance with the Principles of "One Country, Two Systems"

The "one country, two systems" formula was initially put forward for the settlement of the Taiwan issue, but was first successfully implemented in China's resuming the exercise of sovereignty over Hong Kong and Macau, and the process has demonstrated the strong vitality of the formula.

Hong Kong has been part of Chinese territory since the British army invaded and occupied Hong Kong Island during the first Opium War in 1840. According to the *Treaty of Nanking* imposed onto the Qing government by the British in 1842, Hong Kong was ceded to Britain. In 1856, the British and French launched the Second Opium War and compelled the Qing government to conclude the *Convention of Peking* in 1860, which led to the "cession" from China of the southern region of the Kowloon Peninsula. In the wake of the Sino-Japanese war of 1894–1895, Britain forced the Qing government to sign the Convention for the *Extension of Hong Kong Territory* in 1898, according to which the new territories and 262 neighboring islands were leased to Britain for 99 years, which expired on June 30, 1997. The ceding of Hong Kong to Britain was one of the most humiliating episodes in recent Chinese history.

In conformity with the changing international situation, Deng Xiaoping put forward the idea of "one country, two systems" to solve the problem of national reunification after 1978. "One country, two systems" means that, under the one-China premise, the main part of the country keeps its socialist system, while Hong Kong and Macau, as an inalienable party of China, retain their capitalist

On December 19, 1984, Deng Xiaoping met with British Prime Minister Margaret Thatcher and explained the concept of "one country, two systems".

system and way of life for a long period of time to come as special administrative regions.

In accordance to the above policy, the Chinese government and the government of Britain signed, after rounds of negotiation, the Joint Declaration in December 1984, which provided the time, policies and arrangements during the transition for the return of Hong Kong, laying out the rules that both sides agreed upon that could be followed for the final settlement of Hong Kong issue.

In 1985, the Chinese National People's Congress established a Basic Law Drafting Committee for the Hong Kong Special Administrative Region of China. The *Basic Law for the Hong Kong Special Administrative Region* passed in April 1990 set out in clear and concrete terms the provision as to the relations between the Central Government and the Hong Kong Special Administrative Region, the basic rights and obligations of the people in Hong Kong, the political and economic system as well as its foreign affairs in Hong Kong, making good

On December 19, 1984, the state leaders of China and the UK officially signed the Joint Declaration of the Government of the United Kingdom of Great Britain and Northern Ireland and the Government of the People's Republic of China on the Question of Hong Kong.

preparations for China to resume sovereignty over Hong Kong.

In the early days after the signing of the Sino-British Joint Declaration in 1984, the two sides cooperated well and smoothly. However the British-Hong Kong authorities misjudged the situation after the end of the Cold War, went against the spirits of the Joint Declaration and other relevant agreements reached between China and Britain on the arrangements of Hong Kong's return, and prepared to have a "democratic" reform in Hong Kong during the transition or before the PRC resumed sovereignty over Hong Kong. The British intended to establish a "democratic" system in Hong Kong during the last years of British rule so as to retain its political and economic influence in Hong Kong after it was returned to China.

Such policies of the Hong Kong British authorities were rejected resolutely by the Chinese government. At midnight of June 30, 1997 a grand ceremony of Hong Kong's return to China was held at Hong Kong Conference and Exhibition Hall. At the same time the Chinese troops took over Hong Kong's defense duty, starting exercise sovereignty over Hong Kong.

The problem of Macau has similarities with the Hong Kong situation. The Portuguese landed in Macau to engage in trade affairs in 1535 and started to live there in 1557. Portugal forced the Qing government to sign the *Sino-Portuguese Protocol of Lisbon* and *Sino-Portuguese Treaty of Beijing* in March and December of 1887 respectively. Since then the Portuguese have occupied and lived in Macau and treated it as a Portuguese territory. After its formation, the PRC government has stated on many occasions that Macau has always been Chinese territory and that the question of Macau was a question left over from the past. The Chinese government held that the questions should be settled through negotiations when conditions were ripe, and that, pending a settlement, the status quo should be kept for the time being.

The settlement of the Hong Kong questions provided a model for settling the questions of Macau. The Chinese government and the Portuguese government signed a Joint Declaration on Macau in April 1987, which stipulated that the PRC would resume sovereignty over Macau on Dec. 20, 1999.

The *Basic Law for the Macau Special Administrative Region* was passed in March 1993 by the Chinese National People's Congress. On Dec. 19, 1999 the Chinese government and the Portuguese government jointly held a solemn ceremony for the return of Macau to the motherland and China resumed exercise of sovereignty over Macau.

The return of Hong Kong and Macau to the motherland made people in Hong Kong and Macau the true owner of these two areas, put an end to the history of Western colonialists rule in China, and ushered in a new epoch for the development in Hong Kong and Macau.

Ever since their return, Hong Kong and Macau have maintained stable and have developed prosperity under the efficient leadership of the two special administrative regions, with strong support from the Chinese central government. They have embarked on a broad road along which they and the mainland draw on each other's strengths and pursue common development.

In conformity of the underlying goal of upholding China's sovereignty, security and development interests and maintaining long-term prosperity and stability of the two regions, the Central Government of China both adheres to the one-China principle and respects the differences of the two systems, both upholds the power of the central government and ensures a high degree of autonomy in the special administrative regions, both gives play to the role of the mainland as the staunch supporter of Hong Kong and Macau and increases their competitiveness. It implements principle of "one country, two systems, " under which people of Hong Kong govern Hong Kong and people of Macau

On July 1, 1997, the Chinese government resumed the exercise of sovereignty over Hong Kong. The picture is the Hong Kong handover ceremony held by the Chinese government and the British government.

On December 20, 1999, the Chinese government resumed the exercise of sovereignty over Macau. The picture is the Macau handover ceremony held by the Chinese government and Portuguese government.

govern Macau and both regions enjoy a high degree of autonomy. The central government supports the chief executives and governments of the two special administrative regions in governing the two regions in accordance with the law, supports them in leading the people from all walks of life in focusing on economic development, taking effective steps to improve the people's wellbeing, and advancing orderly and phased-in democracy as well as inclusiveness, supports them in promoting the unity of compatriots in Hong Kong and Macau under the banner of loving both the motherland and their respective regions. China opposes any irresponsible remarks or gesticulates on Hong Kong's political system, which is a domestic issue, from outside and guards against and forestalls external intervention in the affairs of Hong Kong and Macau by any country or by forces.

Opposing National Separation, and Safeguarding National Unity

China is a unified, multi-national country, with 56 nationalities in all. All of the nationalities witnessed multi-ethnic fusion during their formation and evolution. During this long historical process, frequent migrations of each nationality resulted in the distribution pattern of China's ethnic groups living together over vast areas while some lived in individual concentrated communities in small areas. The Han people have the largest population, scattering all over the country. In spite of small population and major residence in remote areas, ethnic groups live in the county-level or higher level administrative regions in China. The population distribution characterized by integrated neighborhoods and mutual dependence leads to the fact that it is beneficial for a harmonious and stable inter-ethnic relationship and common development to establish autonomous local governments of ethnic minorities in various types and levels on the basis of concentrated areas of ethnic minorities. This system of regional national autonomy was provided in the *Constitution of People's Republic of China* by 1st National People's Congress in 1954, and was included in the constitution after several amendments.

Facing the sophisticated situation of today, China's diplomacy faces the task of safeguarding national unity and opposing national separation, and Tibet and Xinjiang issues are especially salient.

Tibet is an inseparable part of China and the Tibetan nationality is an important member of the Chinese family of multi-nationalities. Tibetans have lived on the Tibetan plateau for generations and have created a magnificent culture, which is a precious property of the Chinese culture.

The Potala Palace, sitting in the center of Lhasa, is a symbol of the Tibetan history and culture.

Tibet in history was under the despotic feudal serf system marked by the combination of government and religion, which was worse than the system in Europe during the Middle Ages. Although the slave owners accounted for less than 5 percent of the Tibetan population, they owned all of Tibet's means of production and educational resources. Dalai Lama, the head of the Tibetan Buddhism and Tibetan local government, controlled all the religious and administrative power.

Tibet was liberated through peaceful negotiation in 1951. In 1959, a democratic reform was carried out in Tibet, and the despotic feudal serf system marked by combination of government and religion was abolished. The 14th Dalai Lama went in exile abroad. For half a century, the Chinese government has placed great emphasis on the protection and development of Tibetan culture, and has funded large quantities of personnel, materials, and money, with all endeavors, to protect and promote fine traditional cultures in Tibet according to *Constitution of People's Republic of China* and the *Law of Regional National Autonomy*. Meanwhile, the Chinese government has tried its best to enhance modern science and education, which in turn spurs the protection and development of Tibetan culture.

The Dalai clique, shutting its eyes to objective facts and taking religion as its cover, made use of changed international situations to spread the rumor of "extinction of traditional Tibetan culture" in the world, demanding a withdrawal of Chinese army and military facilities from Tibet in an attempt to realize the so-called "Independence of Great Tibetan Zone." In order to draw the attention of the international community, Dalai clique has instigated riots and created social instability, instigated national conflicts, causing serious personal injuries or deaths and heavy property losses in Tibet.

Safeguarding China's territorial and sovereignty integrity is China's core national interest. The Chinese government is firmly against any activities that would separate the country and have Tibetans seek independence. China holds that the Dalai Lama issue is by no means a religious issue, but a political one. The 14th Dalai Lama is more a political refugee engaging in splitting the motherland, rather than a religious figure.

The fundamental difference between Chinese government and the Dalai group is not about being autonomy or not. It has always been a struggle between progress and retrogression, unity and split. The Chinese government is of the view that as long as the Dalai Lama genuinely gives up his divisive stand, stops his activities to split the motherland, abandons any plan to restore the old system in Tibet, dismiss the so-called "Tibetan government in exile" and admits in public that Tibet is an inalienable part of China, and that the government of the P.R.C. is the sole legitimate government representing the whole of China, the central government is willing to contact and negotiate with Dalai Lama for the issue of his personal arrangement in future.

Xinjiang has long been a multi-ethnic region since the ancient times. Today it is home to 55 ethnic groups such as Uygur, Han, Kazak, Hui and Mongolian.

The fact that Tibet is an inalienable part of China has been recognized by all the governments around the world. There is not a single government that has recognized Tibet's "independence" or the so-called "Tibetan government in exile." The so-called Tibet problem was, in the first place, the result of imperialists vainly attempting to carve up China, and to turn China into their colony or semi-colony. After the Dalai clique defected abroad, some anti-China forces have never ceased incitement and support to "Tibetan independence" secession activities by the Dalai clique for even a single minute. Therefore, the so-called Tibet problem is by no means an ethnic minority issue, a religious issue, or a human rights issue, but an issue concerning the Western anti-China forces' conspiracy of containing, splitting, and demonizing China. China is firmly against Dalai's visiting any foreign country to promote activities of splitting China in any capacity, and against any country's providing facilities and forums to Dalai's activities of splitting China.

Xinjiang is also an unalienable part of Chinese territory. Xinjiang Uygur Autonomous Region was founded in 1955. For half a century, Xinjiang has made great progresses in all the aspects of economy and society. After the end of the Cold War, under the influence of religious extremism, ethnic separatism and international terrorism, elements of "East Turkistan Islamic Movement" forces both inside and outside China have resorted to separating and sabotaging activities with terrorist violence as their chief means. They have plotted and organized a number of incidents of terror and violence, seriously jeopardizing the lives, property, and security of the Chinese people of various ethnic groups, and posed a threat to the security and stability of the countries and regions concerned.

After the September 11 event, the calling for international cooperation on the war against terrorism became very strong. In order to get out of their predicament, the "East Turkistan" forces once again raised the banner of "human rights," "freedom of religion" and "interests of ethnic minorities," and have fabricated claims that "the Chinese government is using every opportunity to oppress ethnic minorities." This is done to mislead the public and deceive world opinion in order to escape blows dealt by the international struggle against terrorism. At the same time, they have constantly conspired for various terrorist incidents jeopardizing regional peace and stability, and thus have become the target of the "Shanghai Five" and "Shanghai Cooperation Organization" for regional stability.

In recent years, various separatist forces in Xinjiang have intended to establish a separatist state, the so-called "Eastern Turkistan State" under the banners of "Eastern Turkistan Movement" and have made many terrorist incidents. In particular, the seriously violent incidence of beating, smashing, looting and arson happened on July 5, 2009 in Urumqi, capital of the Xinjiang Uyghur Autonomous Region, jeopardized national unity, social stability and solidarity of different ethnic groups. It disturbed and destroyed the development and progress in Xinjiang and caused great damage to the lives and property of people of all ethnic groups. The Chinese Government has never wavered in its position in opposing such plot to separate the nation.

In September 2002, the UN Security Council included the "East Turkistan Islamic Movement" on its list of terrorist organizations. China has always actively participated in international cooperation against terrorism. China is against any "double standard" on the issue of anti-terrorism, and strongly opposes any support by any country in any pretext to any terrorist activities and activities intending to split the country.

China's Multilateral Diplomacy

The relationship between contemporary China and the world has witnessed such a historic change that China's future has been bound up with that of the world. China is promoting the world's development and prosperity by its own development and prosperity, and playing a constructive role in maintaining world peace and advancing human progress with a responsible attitude. China's active participation in multilateral diplomacy, playing a constructive role in international affairs, and pushing forward a more just and rational international order have become the most active aspects of China's foreign relations.

Comprehensively Participating in International Institutions, and Actively Promoting Multilateral Diplomacy

In the evolution of world history, conflicts and wars occurred among some ancient civilizations, leading to the wax and wane as well as the fusion among some civilizations and the disappearance of others. The Chinese civilization is remarkable in that it has, in general, maintained its main characteristics and integrity unchallenged though it has rubbed elbows with others in history. This is due to the fact that the Chinese civilization was separated in the Southwest by the Himalayas from the Indian civilization, and by vast deserts and plateaus in Northwest from those in Middle East and Europe. The Chinese civilization has been the only one of the four great civilizations that has survived and continued until today.

In recent history, the West became strong economically after they led in industrialization, and promoted the global economic integration and cultural collisions and fusions. China's door was forced open by West countries with warships and cannons, reducing China to a semi-colonial and semi-feudal country from a "Celestial Empire." During this bloody process of humiliation, a fair number of people with lofty ideals carried out various attempts to rescue China's destiny. The Westernization Movement characterized by "Chinese learning for essence and Western for practical use" failed after the Sino-Japanese war (1894). The reform movement of 1898 lasted only for 100 days before its abortion. The Revolution of 1911 succeeded in overthrowing the feudal ruling but still failed to change China's international status of humiliation. China was in the end drawn into the international system passively and landed in a subordinated position.

Led by the Communist Party of China, the Chinese people of all nationalities successfully overthrew the rule of imperialism, feudalism and bureaucratic capitalism, won the great victory of the new-democratic revolution and founded the People's Republic of China in 1949 after waging hard, protracted and tortuous struggles. New China's government hoped that China could establish relations with Western countries based on the principle of equality and mutual respect, and that China could participate in the international community and render its contribution to world peace and prosperity.

Soon after the founding of New China, then-Premier and Foreign Minister Zhou Enlai sent a telegraph to then-UN Secretary General Lie, demanding that the UN expel the representatives of the Taiwan authorities, and informed the UN that New China had appointed Zhang Wentian as the permanent representative of China to the UN. Due to US obstruction, China's demand was not accepted. After

In October 1971, the lawful seat of the People's Republic of China in the United Nations was restored at the 26th session of the UN General Assembly.

the Korean War, the United States manipulated the United Nations to shelve the discussion of China's legitimate seat in the UN under the pretext of the Korean War. Constrained by the division of international political forces and Cold War confrontation, China's contacts with the international community were initially limited to its relations with the Soviet Union, East European socialist countries, and a few neighboring countries.

After the deterioration of Sino-Soviet relations in 1960s, China was not only in confrontation with Western countries in the international system, but its relations with socialist countries were terribly affected. In the wake of the "Cultural Revolution," China was once again trapped in isolation in the international community as China withdrew from the few international organizations that it had only just joined, and even ceased to participate in some international sports contests for a while.

On November 10, 2011, the fourth WTO Ministerial Conference was held inDoha, the capital of Qatar. This conference reviewed and unanimously adopted the decision on China's accession to the WTO.

The 1970s witnessed changes in the relationship between China and the international system. On Oct. 26, 1971, the United Nations General Assembly adopted at its 26th Session Resolution 1758, which restored the seat and all the lawful rights of the government of the PRC in the United Nations, and landmarked an important step of China's participation in international organizations and integration into the international system. By 1977, China had joined 21 international organizations including the UN, and had signed off on 45 international treaties, agreements and conventions.

The year of 1978 was a turning point in China's history. China began to practice an opening-up policy, which was carried out gradually from the coast areas to the interior of China. While "inviting in," China took an active step of "going out" by actively participating in the activities of the UN, starting the process of integration into the international system. In the realm of the economy, China joined the World Bank and the International Monetary Fund (IMF) in 1980, and resumed its observer status in the General Agreement and Tariff and Trade (GATT) in 1982. China formally applied for the restoration of its contracting party status in GATT in 1986. In the realm of security, China began, in 1980, to participate in the Conference on Disarmament in Geneva and its affiliated special committees and working groups. By the end of 1986, China had joined the UN and all of its affiliated multilateral organizations. The *Report on the Work of the Government* delivered to the 4th Session of the Sixth National People's Congress stated that "China supports the work undertaken by the UN in the spirit of the Charter and participates in activities for world peace and development sponsored by the organization and its specialized agencies. China has joined a wide range of international organizations, actively engaged in multilateral diplomacy and strived to promote international cooperation in all fields." This statement signaled a change in China's policies regarding multilateral international mechanisms represented by the UN, which meant more participation.

The end of Cold War removed the political obstacles of exchanges between the East and the West, and the world economy was integrated into a whole. Globalization has blurred the border between domestic and international issues, and many problems facing human-kind, such as environmental problems, epidemic diseases, energy deficiency, migrant problems, and trans-boundary crimes, are becoming convergent, and they are no longer problems that a single country can solve. In security areas, the end of the Cold War erased the possibility of large-scale wars between superpowers. On the one hand the international situation relaxed in general, but on the other hand, various traditional security problems are still far from being solved while non-traditional security problems become prominent. Multilateral co-operations on international security issues are an important field of multilateral diplomacy in post-Cold War era. Demands for the international community to reinforce coordination and broaden cooperation to address the common challenges have been on the rise. International organizations are becoming more important and multilateral diplomacy has become more active than ever before.

In June 2001, the state leaders of China, Russia, Kazakhstan, Kyrgyzstan, Tajikistan and Uzbekistan held the first meeting and signed the *Declaration of the Establishment of the Shanghai Cooperation Organization*.

Facing the environment of globalization in the post-Cold War era, China has unswervingly followed the policy of opening-up, adapted itself to the trend of economic globalization, and actively participated in international economic cooperation and competition. While making full use of the beneficial conditions and opportunities of economic globalization, China is fully aware of the risks that result from economic globalization. China has joined more international regimes and energetically expanded its multilateral diplomacy, making it more integrated into the international community with remarkable accomplishments in this regard.

By 2008 China has joined more than 130 intergovernmental organizations and thousands of non-governmental international organizations, including such global international organizations as the UN, G8+5 and G20, regional international organizations such as the "Shanghai Cooperation Organization" and ASEAN+3 Dialogue Mechanism, and trans-regional international organizations

In November 2006, Forum on China–Africa Cooperation was held in Beijing.

as the Asian-European Summit, APEC and China-Africa Cooperation Forum. By 2008, China has signed or acceded to 300 multilateral international treaties, conventions, agreement and protocols from 157 in 1989, covering the fields of politics, security, economy, culture and so on.

While integrating into the international community, China has followed an open strategy of mutual benefit and win-win. This strategy calls for China to promote regional and global development by its own development, and extend the convergence of interests with other parties. In participating in international organizations, China has maintained multilateralism and open regionalism. As a developing country, China has actively engaged in summit diplomacy, advocated China's views, expanded its relations with other countries, and taken due responsibilities and obligations while safeguarding China's interests and improving its global image. China has played a constructive role in solving global and regional problems in an active way. For instance, China has spearheaded the Bo'ao Forum, promoted the establishment of the Shanghai Cooperative Organization, actively promoted and hosted the six-party talks on the Korean nuclear issue. China has gradually changed its mode of passive participation in multilateral organizations, becoming an active participator, an advocator, and a leader in multilateral diplomacy.

The relationship between contemporary China and the world has undergone historic changes. China's economy has been a vital component of the world economy and China has become an important member of the international system. China's future has been bound up with that of the world. China cannot realize its development while being isolated from the world, and the world cannot have its prosperity and stability without China. China is promoting the world's development by its own development and contributing its own prosperity to that of the world.

Playing a Constructive Role in the United Nations

The United Nations is the most universal, representative and authoritative inter-governmental organization in the world. With a more than tripled expansion, its members have grown from 51 at its founding to today's 192, and its activities and functions now cover politics, economy, security, human rights, and other social affairs in post-Cold War era.

As one of the founding members of the UN and one of the permanent members of the United Nations Security Council, China has placed great emphasis on the role of the UN, participated actively in the UN's work in all aspects and all fields, and rendered its full support to the role of the UN.

In September 2000, during the United Nations Millennium Summit, heads of the five permanent members met under the initiative of China.

In March 2004, the international conference of the United Nations Millennium Development Goals was held in Beijing.

After China had its legitimate seat in UN restored, China sent high-ranking delegates to the annual general assembly meeting, elaborating China's stances and views on global and regional issues. With the enhancing role of the UN in international affairs after the Cold War, Chinese leaders have attended all the important meetings within the UN framework.

Chinese then-President Jiang Zemin was present at the United Nations Millennium Summit in 2000 and elaborated to the world the Chinese government's support of the organization. He stated that the active role of the UN must be strengthened, not weakened, and its authority defended, not jeopardized, under the new situation. China firmly has defended the purposes and principles of the *UN Charter*, and will continue its support to the UN and its Security Council to play an active role in handling international affairs and safeguarding world peace with all its member states enjoying equal rights in participating in world affairs.

Then-President Hu Jintao was present at the Conference in Commemoration of the 60th anniversary of the founding of the UN in 2005. He proposed at the conference that the UN and other multilateral mechanisms should further play their constructive role in solving international disputes, maintaining peace, providing humanitarian aid, and many other fields. He also elaborated China's diplomatic thoughts of "building a harmonious world of enduring peace and common prosperity."

The United Nations is a big stage for all countries to conduct consultation and cooperation with each other. It is also a big family where people of all countries are brought together. China firmly promotes reform of the global governance system with the United Nations at its core. China firmly upholds the role and authority of the United Nations, supports the United Nations in renewing and improving itself in keeping with a changing world, and looks forward to a United Nations that plays a bigger role in international affairs. China is ready to deepen cooperation with the United Nations and get more actively involved in UN activities in various fields and has played an increasingly important, positive and constructive role in maintaining world peace, and settling international and regional hotspot issues under the framework of the UN. Examples include China's participation in the UN peacekeeping operations, promoting arms control and disarmament, and cooperation in human rights affairs within the framework of the UN, among others.

Participation in the UN Peace-keeping operations

Peacekeeping operations are one of the important means for the UN to perform its duty in maintaining international peace and security. The *UN Charter* stipulates that one of the major roles of the UN is to maintain international peace and security, and "to that end: to take effective collective measures for the prevention and removal of threats to peace, and for the suppression of acts of aggression or other breaches of the peace, and to bring about by peaceful means,

and in conformity with the principles of justice and international law, adjustment or settlement of international disputes or situations which might lead to a breach of the peace."

Since the 36th general assembly of the UN in 1981, China has adopted a positive attitude towards the role of the UN peacekeeping operations in relaxing tensions and favored in principle peacekeeping operations according to the *UN charter*. China began to pay its due to UN peace-keeping operations in 1982 and became a member of the UN Special Committee on Peacekeeping Operations in 1988. In 2001, China established its peace-keeping office with its Defense Ministry, and participated in the Class-A Stand-by Mechanism arrangement for the UN peace-keeping operation. In December 2013, China began to dispatch organic security and peacekeeping troops to Mali. By 2013, China has dispatched 22,000 military personnel to 24 UN peacekeeping missions with

In December 2013, China sent the first peace-keeping force (PKF) to Mali. It is the 24th UN peacekeeping operations that China attended since it sent UN peacekeepers in 1990 for the first time, and also the first time that China sent troops to participate in the peacekeeping operations.

Chronicle of China's Events in UN Peacekeeping	
In January 1982	China began to pay its due to the UN peacekeeping operations.
In April 1989	China joined the special committee on Peacekeeping Operations.
In November 1989	China sent non-military personnel to the UN peacekeeping operations for the first time.
In April 1990	China sent military observers to the UN peacekeeping operations for the first time.
In April 1992	China sent non-combat units to serve in UN peacekeeping operations.
In January 2000	China first sent civilian police to UN peacekeeping operations.
In January 2002	China formally participated in the Class-A stand-by arrangements mechanism for the UN peace-keeping operations.
In September 2007	the Chinese major general Zhao Jingmin was designated as commander in chief for United Nations mission for referendum in Western Sahara, and became the first Chinese serviceman serving as a senior commander of UN peacekeeping force.
In December 2013	China began to dispatch organic security and peacekeeping troops.

9 officers and soldiers have laid down their lives performing such duties and nearly 2000 officers and soldiers are performing their duties on various peace-keeping missions in the world today. China is now the biggest troop and police contributor among the five permanent members of the UN Security Council. It also contributes the largest share of UN peacekeeping costs among all developing countries.

China holds that the UN shall play an irreplaceable role in peacekeeping, which should adhere to the purposes and principles of the UN Charter and other universally recognized norms of international relations, especially the principles of respecting the sovereignty of all countries and non-interference in other countries' internal affairs, obtaining agreement from the country concerned beforehand, neutrality and non-use of force except for self-defense. China believes that these principles guarantee that peacekeeping missions will be smoothly and successfully carried out.

Promoting disarmament within the United Nations framework

China is one of the five permanent members of the UN Security Council and a nuclear power. Since the very day China had nuclear weapons, it has adhered to the policy of no-first-use of nuclear weapons at any time and in any circumstances, and made commitment that under no circumstances will it use or threaten to use nuclear weapons against non-nuclear-weapon states or nuclear-weapon-free zones. China advocated for negotiating and concluding a legally-binding international instrument in this regard at an early date.

Since 1980, China has formally joined in the work of the Geneva Conference on Disarmament and its sub-committees and working groups, and actively attended meetings of the First Committee of the United Nations General Assembly, which considers issues on disarmament and international security. China has been present at the annual conference of the Disarmament Commission of the UN. China has supported the United Nations' important role in non-proliferation. China has so far acceded to all the international treaties on non-proliferation, joined in the relevant international organizations, and has so far established a comprehensive legal system for export control of nuclear, biological, chemical, and missile and related dual-use items and technologies. China has spared no effort in strengthening law enforcement in the field of non-proliferation export control has fulfilled its international obligations and promotes the arms control process in both chemical and conventional weapon areas in an active and steady manner.

In the realm of conventional weapons control, China has earnestly fulfilled its obligations under the Convention on *Certain Conventional Weapons (CCW)* and its additional protocols. It has taken concrete measures to ensure that its anti-personnel landmines in service meet the relevant technical requirements of the *Amended Protocol on Landmines* and strictly abides by the domestic arms export laws and regulations and relevant UNSC resolutions, and does not transfer weapons to conflict regions or non-state actors. China took part in the negotiation process of the *Arms Trade Treaty* and remains engaged with all parties on the follow-up work of this Treaty and makes joint efforts to build a regulated and reasonable international arms trade order.

On the newly emerged cybersecurity issue, China holds all countries should safeguard common security through practical cooperation on the basis of mutual respect and considers the top priority is to formulate international rules of cyberspace under the UN framework. To this end, China and the U.S. maintain communications within the framework of China-US Strategic and Economic Dialogue. China, Russia and some other countries jointly put forward the "International Code of Conduct for Information Security" to the UNGA in 2011, and China stands ready to work with other parties to achieve an early

In September 1996, Qian Qichen, Vice Premier and Minister of Foreign Affairs, signed the Comprehensive Nuclear Test Ban Treaty in the UN Headquarters in New York on behalf of the People's Republic of China.

On August 21, 2001, China Arms Control and Disarmament Association was set up in Beijing. This is the first non-governmental organization of the arms control field.

consensus on the Code of Conduct and jointly build a peaceful, secure, open and cooperative cyberspace.

In addition, China has taken big steps to reduce its military personnel and increase its military transparency. After the Central Military Committee of the Chinese government decided to cut its military personnel by 1 million in 1985, it decided to cut another half a million in three years from 1997. A third cut was made in 2003 by another 200,000 in two years, making China's total military force now 2.3 million.

Promoting human rights within the framework of the UN and international cooperation on human rights issues

One of the principal aims of the United Nations is to promote and encourage the respect for human rights and fundamental freedom of human beings, and protecting and promoting human rights are the goals of the *United Nations Charters*.

China began to participate in the United Nations human rights conference as an observer in 1979, and was elected to the Human Rights Commission in the Economic and Social Council of the United Nations in 1981. China has been elected to the Human Rights Commission since 1982 and has participated in the annual meetings ever since then and has enthusiastically promoted international cooperation in human rights. China supports the programs of the UN's Office of the High Commissioner for Human Rights (OHCHR), and made donations of US$ 20,000, US$ 30,000, and US$ 50,000 to it from in 2010, 2011 and 2012 respectively. In 2011 China and the OHCHR jointly held the China-UN Legal Seminar and discussed such issues as death penalty reform trend in the world.

After the end of the Cold War, some countries made use of the human rights issue to criticize and interfere in other countries' internal affairs, making human rights issues one of the focal contradictions between the North and the South. China is against interference in any country's international affair in the name of human rights but maintains bilateral dialogues with relevant countries on the basis of equality and mutual respect. China has held human rights dialogues with the European Union, Australia, Canada, the United States, Norway, Great Britain, Germany, and Switzerland. It also has sent legal experts to have dialogues with their US counterparts, held the EU-China Human Rights Seminar and conducted technical cooperation projects on human rights with Australia. From 2010 to 2012, the China Society for Human Rights Studies, together with some other organizations, held the third, fourth and fifth sessions of the Beijing Forum on Human Rights, discussing the relations between human rights and development, culture, science and technology and the environment. The Forum has become an important stage for international human rights dialogues and exchanges involving both developing and developed countries.

China has participated in international cooperation on human rights within the framework of the UN and the Chinese government has joined 27 international human rights conventions, including the *International Covenant on Economic, Social and Cultural Rights*, and actively works for the approval of the *International Covenant on Civil and Political Rights*. The Chinese government has taken active measures to guarantee the implementation of its obligations as stipulated by the international human rights conventions it has joined and has regularly submitted to the UN reports of its implementation of the relevant treaties. Within the UN Human Right Commission. China supports the reform of UN human rights bodies with more democracy and transparency. The essence

On November 12, 2013, UN General Assembly re-elected members of the United Nations Human Rights Council and China was overwhelmingly elected for a term from 2014 to 2016.

of the reform is de-politicizing human rights issues, rejecting double standards, replacing Cold War mentality with equal dialogues of mutual respect in human rights. China proposed that human rights issues should be handled with balanced views so as to properly handle the relationship between the universality and speciality of human rights, that the choices of different countries in protecting and promoting human rights should be respected so as to increase dialogue and learn from each other on human rights issue.

China sets great store by human rights issue and chapter II article 33 of the *PRC Constitution* provides "the State respects and preserves human rights." It has promulgated or revised many of its laws to protect and promote its human rights condition. China is not against the discussions of human rights issues with other countries on an equal footing and with mutual respect, but is against the interference in China's internal affairs with the excuse of human rights, as well as the politicization of human rights issue in the UN Human Rights Commission. In order to enhance international communications and exchanges, China has published white papers to explain to the world the efforts and the progresses China has made in protecting and promoting human rights since 1991. These white papers include *Human Rights Situation in China* (1991), *China's Progresses in Human Rights* (1995), *Progress in China's Human Rights Cause in 1996* (1997), *Freedom of Religious Belief in China* (1997), *New Progress in Human Rights in the Tibet Autonomous Region* (1998), *Fifty Years of Progress in China's Human Rights* (2000), *Progress in China's Human Rights Causes in 2000* (2001), *Progress in China's Human Rights Cause in 2003* (2004), *China's Progress in Human Rights in 2004* (2005), *Progress in China's Human Rights in 2009* (2010), *Progress in China's Human Rights in 2012* (2013), etc.

Supporting the UN reform

In order to better adapt to the changes with the international situation and increase the efficiency of the UN, China has supported the UN reform. The

Chinese government issued *China's Position Paper on UN Reforms*, which laid out China's policy on UN reform in a systematic and comprehensive way. The paper states: Reforms should be in the interest of multilateralism, and enhance the UN's authority and efficiency, as well as its capacity to deal with new threats and challenges. Reforms should be all-dimensional and multi-sectoral, and should aim to succeed in both aspects of security and development; especially, reforms should aim at reversing the trend of the "UN giving priority to security over development"; Reforms shall accommodate the propositions and concerns of all UN members, especially those of the developing countries.

On the core issue of UN reform—the reform of the United Nations Security Council—China proposes: The reform with the UN Security Council is multifaceted encompassing the enlargement of the UN Security Council and the increases with its efficiency; The reform should be conducive to enhancing

In June 2013, President Xi Jinping met with UN Secretary-General Ban Ki-moon in Beijing.

the authority and efficiency of the Council, and strengthening its capacity to deal with global threats and challenges; Increasing the representation of developing countries should be given priority; The principle of geographic balance should be adhered to, with representation of different cultures and civilizations taken into consideration.

Playing a Responsible Role in the Settlement of Global Issues

As China rises in its power and becomes more integrated with the international community, the Chinese government has proactively participated in the coordination and cooperation within the international society, lived its obligations, and shared the responsibility of a big power in maintaining world security and promoting global development.

Handling the global economic issues with a strong sense of responsibility

As economic globalization has made the world economy intimately connected, an economic crisis or recession in any form would have negative repercussions on a global scale. Since its opening-up, China's export-oriented economy has made China's economy and the world economy so intertwined as to make them an inseparable whole. All global economic crises have had great negative impacts on the Chinese economy. However, China is convinced that under globalization, China's economy cannot sustain fast development without the development and prosperity of the world economy as well as the rise of its neighbors; and China has realized that helping others is helping itself. When a regional or global economic crisis happens, China is ready to bear the cost and undertake its responsibility and plays a very positive role. For instance, China found its economy under great pressure when China's Southeast Asian neighbors were struck with a serious financial crisis in 1997. Surmounting many difficulties, domestically China maintained the stability of its RMB and increased its domestic consumption. Internationally China not only provided large amounts

In September 2013, President Xi Jinping attended the 8th Summit of G20 Leaders and said that all countries should strive to shape a world economy, where all countries enjoy development and innovation, growth linkage, and interests integration.

of economic aids to those Southeast Asian countries seriously hit through bilateral arrangements but also provided multilateral assistance to them through International Monetary Funds. China's efforts helped Southeast Asian countries overcome the crisis and won trust from its neighbors.

Since its participation in the World Trade Organization (WTO) in 2001, China has adhered to the principle of a balance between rights and obligations while strictly following the WTO rules to fulfill its obligations. China have lived up to its commitments by lowering tariffs and reducing other trade barriers, revising its domestic laws and regulations, expanding the areas opening to the outside, increasing the degree of free trade in commodities, enlarging trade openness in the service industry, stepping up intellectual property rights protection, increasing transparency in trade policies, and more. Within the WTO, China stands for perfecting the international trade and financial system, promoting free trade and open investment, and the settlement of trade frictions through coordination and cooperation.

The subprime lending crisis that started in the U.S. in 2008 has caused an international financial crisis, which has inflicted a far-reaching impact on the world economy and has taken a heavy toll on the Chinese economy. In order to cope with the challenges posed by the financial crisis, the Chinese government has swiftly made adjustments with its macro-economic policy and formulated a proactive fiscal policy and moderately easy monetary policy with a stimulus package that focuses on expanding domestic demand aimed at driving economic growth through both consumption and investment. Domestically China accelerated investment, giving priority to projects affecting people's well-being, infrastructure, and environmental protection. Globally, China has vigorously participated in international cooperation. China has opposed trade and investment protectionism, calling for countries to maintain confidence, enhance communications, and render mutual supports. China has called for the following measures to be taken: enhancing and improving IMF's surveillance over the macro-economic policies of the economies of the major reserve currencies; improving the governing body of the IMF and the World Bank; streamlining the international monetary system so as to enhance surveillance over the issuing and administrating mechanisms of the major reserve currencies; stabilizing exchange rates between the major reserve currencies; pluralizing and rationalizing the international monetary system. Since the outbreak of the global financial crisis in 2008, China has not only made contribution to the IMF and extended a helping hand to countries in difficulty, but also resorted to its own steady and robust growth and together with other emerging market countries, sustained hope for global economic recovery.

At the G20 summit in 2013, Chinese President Xi Jinping also brought up a series of new ideas on development innovation, growth linkage and interests integration, and advocated the establishment of partnership among G20 members to build the awareness of community of common destiny, cooperating in competitions, and achieving win-win results in cooperation.

International cooperation on the global war on terrorism

The "September 11" attack against the U.S. has upgraded terrorism from an ordinary non-traditional issue to a public hazard of the world. Taking strict precautions against and opposing terrorism have become major new tasks of national security and strategy facing major countries of the world.

China has been a victim of terrorism. "Eastern Turkistan Islamic Movement" and other terrorist groups have made terrorist attacks in China's Xinjiang Autonomous Region, resulting in injuries and deaths as well as damages to property, seriously jeopardizing the stability and the security of the lives and property of people of different ethnic groups in the area. In coping with this public hazard, China has made its policy on anti-terrorism in conformity with the new concept of security featuring "mutual trust, mutual benefit, equality, and coordination" and joined international efforts in fighting global terrorism.

Chinese and foreign troops in the multilateral anti-terrorism military exercise.

China holds that the war against terrorism should be conducted in a comprehensive way to address both the root causes and symptoms with a focus on rooting out the causes of terrorism. Fighting terrorism should have concrete evidence and a clear target in conformity with the purpose and principle of the *UN Charter* and other universally accepted international norms, and give a leading role to the United Nations and its Security Council. Terrorism should not be linked to any specific nation or religion and fighting terrorism should avoid double standards. The international community should make joint efforts to resolutely condemn and fight against terrorism in all forms regardless of their targets, places and manifestations.

China forcefully supports and takes part in international anti-terrorism cooperation. China has acceded to the *International Convention for the Suppression of Terrorist Bombings* and signed the *International Convention for the Suppression of the Financing of Terrorism*. China has joined 10 and signed one of the 12 international anti-terror conventions. China and other members of the Shanghai Cooperative Organization have signed the *Shanghai Convention against Terrorism, Separatism and Extremism* in 2001. According to the spirit of the convention, SCO established the Regional Anti-Terrorism Structure (RATS) in Tashkent, capital of Uzbekistan, as the permanent cooperative organ for its members to fight against the "three forces" and cooperate in other security areas. So far China has held several bilateral as well as multilateral joint military exercises with other members of SCO, institutionalized within the SCO in joint military exercise in opposing terrorism.

China has conducted consultations and exchanges with the U.S., Russia, Britain, France, Pakistan, India, and more than 30 countries on counter-terrorism. China has actively participated in the UN Security Council's Commission on Fighting Terrorism. China motivated the APEC Shanghai summit to issue a statement on fighting terrorism. China also led the heads of government, Ministers of Defense, heads of the law-enforcement ministries, as well as foreign

In May 2011, Tianshan No.2 joint anti-terrorism exercise of SCO state members was held in Kashi, Xinjiang. The picture is Armed Force Anti-terrorism Forces of China under review.

ministers of the members of Shanghai Cooperative Organization (SCO) to issue a joint statement on fighting terrorism. China has conducted anti-terrorism joint military exercises within the framework of the SCO, including the Sino-Kyrgyzstani joint anti-terrorism military exercise in October 2002, and the first multilateral military exercise against terrorism with Kazakhstan, Kirgizstan, Russia and Tajikistan in China's Xinjiang and Kazakhstan in August 2003. In 2006, China and Kazakhstan held "Tianshan-I" joint counter-terrorism military exercise. China and Russia had joint anti-terrorism exercise "Cooperation-2007" between Chinese military police and Russian police of Ministry of Internal Affairs. In 2011 the law enforcement agencies of the SCO member states held a joint counterterrorism exercise "Tianshan-2" at Kashgar Xinjiang Autonomous Region.

Actively participating in the programs of international community in dealing with climate changes

Global climate change and its adverse effects are a common concern of mankind. Fully aware of the importance and urgency of addressing climate change, China set store by addressing climate change issues. Taking into overall consideration of both economic development and ecological construction, the Chinese government has participated in international climate cooperation on climate issue and increased its efforts addressing climate change issues.

China has actively participated in the process of international negotiation on climate change, such as the 13th Conference of the Parties and the 3rd Meeting of the Parties at Bali in December 2007, the Copenhagen Climate Change Conference in 2009, Cancun Conference in 2010, Durban Conference in 2011, Doha Conference in 2012 and the Warsaw Conference in 2013. Chinese leaders have availed many bilateral and multilateral occasions to elaborate China's

In November 2013, Warsaw Climate Change Conference 2013 was concluded. Xie Zhenhua, head of the Chinese delegation, is receiving interview of media.

position on international cooperation on climate change. In accordance to the principle of "mutual benefit and win-win cooperation, being practical and effective," "common but differentiated responsibilities," China promoted for "finding equilibrium between the interest of different countries and the interest of the world."

China has acceded to more than 50 international treaties or conventions on environment protections and faithfully lived up to its obligations, including the *United Nations Framework Convention on Climate Change* and the *Kyoto Protocol, Montreal Protocol on Substances that Deplete the Ozone Layer, Stockholm Convention on Persistent Organic Pollutants, Convention on Biological Diversity, United Nations Convention to Combat Desertification*, and more.

China actively participates in and promotes international cooperation on handling climate change, and enhances consultation and dialogue with other countries to explore for common programs to address the issue of climate change. China not only held consultation with the United States, the European Union, Denmark, Japan and other developed countries and regions but also enhanced communications with other developing countries, promoting the establishment of a consultation mechanism among the BASIC countries, and coordinating and promoting the process of climate change talks by adopting the "BASIC plus" framework. China urged developed countries to demonstrate their sincerity and live up to their promises to cut their emission more forcefully and to provide support in capitals, technology and capability building to developing countries.

China energetically develops cooperation in research on climate change with foreign governments, international organizations and research institutes. China actively participates in international scientific cooperation programs, including the World Climate Research Program (WCRP) under the framework of the Earth System Science Partnership (ESSP), International Geosphere-Biosphere Program (IGBP), Global Climate Observation System (GCOS), Global Ocean Observation

System (GOOS), Array for Real-Time Geostrophic Oceanography (ARGO) and International Polar Year. In addition, China enhances information exchanges and resources sharing with relevant international organizations and institutes. Up to July 20, 2008, China had 244 cooperation projects on the Clean Development Mechanism (CDM) cooperation projects successfully registered with the United Nations, which were expected to reduce carbon dioxide emissions by 113 million tons annually.

Promoting the Settlement of Regional Hot Issues

After the end of the Cold War, the international situation relaxed in general but regional hot spots and conflicts remain common jeopardizing regional stability. At the same time, earthquakes, tsunamis and other natural disasters have frequently caused damages to the living and development of human-kind.

Whenever a country was struck by natural disaster, the Chinese government has always been ready to provide humanitarian assistance to help those victimized to overcome their difficulties. For instance, when the Indian Ocean earthquake and tsunami caused disastrous consequences in 2004, the Chinese government and people undertook the biggest foreign assistance campaign since the founding of the PRC by providing timely and sincere rescue and assistances to the tsunami-hit countries for disaster relief and reconstruction. In the settlement of regional hot spots, the Chinese government has followed international principles, spoken out for justice by playing a constructive role that facilitated the proper settlement of these issues.

On the Middle East issue

The Middle East issue or the conflicts between Arab countries, including Palestine, and Israel have brought the two sides to three large-scale wars since 1947, making nearly 1 million Palestinians homeless refugees. The conflicts between Arabs and Israelis have been escalating, making it the regional hot issue lasting for the longest time in the world.

China has always been sympathetic with the misfortunes of the Palestinian people and has resolutely supported the struggle of Arabic and Palestinian

In May 2013, President Xi Jinping of China held talks with Palestinian President Mahmoud Abbas in Beijing.

people for recovering their lost land and restoring their national right. China has supported the Palestinians to return to their homeland and supported their right to reestablish an independent state. As early as 1988, China recognized the State of Palestine and established diplomatic ties with it. On the other hand, China are not against the Jewish nation or the Israeli people, and does not support the idea to annihilate the state of Israel.

The Palestine issue is the core of the Middle East Issue. So long as the legitimate national rights and interests of the Palestinian people cannot be restored, peace between Palestine and Israel would not be realized, let alone peace and stability in the region. The history of and reality in the Middle East has shown that force cannot solve the problem, and confrontation has been only detrimental to the settlement of the issue. China has supported the Middle East peace process, dispatched its special envoy for Middle East affairs, and made its efforts and due contribution to the progress in the Middle East peace process.

Soon after it was formed in 2013, the New Chinese administration invited both the Palestinian and Israeli leaders to visit China. Xi Jinping raised four-point proposal on resolving Palestine issue during his meeting with Palestinian President Mahmoud Abbas: the right direction to follow should be an independent Palestinian State and peaceful co-existence of Palestine and Israel; negotiation should be taken as the only way to peace between Palestine and Israel; principles such as "land for peace" should be firmly upheld; the international community should provide important guarantee for progress in the peace process.

China has held that the parties concerned should settle the Jerusalem issue, the crux and most difficult part of the Middle East issue, through negotiation based on the relevant UN resolutions, and unilateral actions should be avoided that go against the settlement of the issue.

On the Afghanistan issue

Afghanistan is China's close neighbor and one of the first few countries that established diplomatic ties with China soon after the PRC was founded. As the only Afghan neighbor that does not have any unsettled issue left over from history with Afghanistan, China has always supported the Afghan people's righteous causes of national liberation and national sovereignty.

After the "September 11" incident in 2001, Afghanistan became the focus of international attention as the center of the U.S. counter-terrorist war turned to this country. As a close neighbor of Afghanistan, China hopes that Afghanistan becomes a peaceful country, a country that can cooperate with the international community, and a country where different ethnic groups can live together in peace. China advocates that the international community should support an "Afghan-led and Afghan-owned" process of peace and reconstruction; respect the right of the Afghan government and people to determine their own destiny; help Afghanistan enhance sovereignty, ownership and development capacity; support Afghanistan in capacity building so that it can take over the responsibility of safeguarding national peace and stability at an early date; support Afghanistan in advancing national reconciliation through its own efforts; support advancing

reconciliation through its own effort; support Afghanistan in developing its economy; and support Afghanistan in developing external relations on the basis of mutual respect, equality and mutual benefit.

The Afghan peace process has been undergoing for 10 years since 2003. With strong support from the international community and the unremitting efforts of the Afghan government and people, encouraging achievements have been accomplished. China has vigorously supported the efforts of Afghan government and people in maintaining stability in their country, developing their economy, and national reconstruction after peace is returned to the country. China has rendered aids to Afghanistan in the forms of material, cash, and preferential loans, and has joined the international community to push forward Afghan reconstruction and promote peace and stability by enthusiastically participating in the construction of such infrastructure as roads, water conservancies and hospitals in Afghanistan. In the past 10 years, China has established hospitals,

In September 2013, China and Afghanistan signed an economic and technological cooperation agreement.

schools, irrigation works, and other projects of people's livelihood for Afghanistan. In 2011 China decided to provide another RMB 150 million worth of aid gratis to Afghanistan.

On the issue of Darfur in Sudan

Due to drought and desertification in the west part of Sudan, conflicts and competitions for water and grass land between different tribes began to take place in the 1960s and 1970s among the farmers and herdsman, leading to the deterioration in the regional situation, which culminated in the large-scale conflicts between the anti-government troops and the government forces, making Darfur a hot spot catching the attention of the international community.

China has advocated at United Nations Security Council that the sovereignty and territorial integrity of Sudan should be respected and the Darfur issue should be settled through political means by equal dialogue and consultation. Pressures or sanctions, or threatening with force, should be avoided. China has held that the measures that the United Nations Security Council takes should reflect the common wishes of the international society, address the legitimate concerns of the Sudanese government, and take the final and proper settlement of the issue as the basis. The international community should help Sudan in improving the humanitarian and security situation in Darfur, and provide assistance in reconstruction and development so as to realize peace, stability and development in the Darfur area as early as possible. While trying to settle the Darfur issue, the international community should give full play to the leading role to the UN-African Union-Sudanese government trilateral mechanism, with a balanced consideration for peace keeping and the political settlement of the Darfur issue.

In consideration of the long-term stability and development in Sudan, China has provided constructive suggestions and advices to the Sudanese government and facilitated the communication and coordination between the Sudanese government and related parties. The Chinese government has dispatched its

China's PKF implemented the free clinics programs in South Sudan.

special envoy to Darfur in 2007, which has paid visits to Sudan and other related countries including those in Europe, American, some African countries, as well as the United Nations, African Union, Arab Union, and EU headquarters. China has maintained close contacts and exchanges with, and persuaded on different occasions, related parties to narrow their differences, increase mutual trust and reduce suspicion of each other so as to reach an agreement on the deployment of "Joint Mission" in Darfur along with the African Union and the United Nations. China, as the chair of the United Nations Security Council in July 2007, has pushed forward in the United Nations Security Council to pass the 1769 resolution unanimously, attaining a first-stage achievement in the efforts of the international community to settle the Darfur issue. At the request of the United Nations, China committed to send 315 multi-functional engineer corps to join the peace-keeping missions in Darfur. In addition, China has provided several packages of humanitarian aids to Darfur and has enthusiastically participated in the reconstruction and economic development in Darfur.

According to the *Comprehensive Peace Agreement* between the South and North parts of Sudan signed on January 9, 2005, South Sudan held a referendum on its own future. China dispatched delegation to observe the referendum at the invitation of both South and North Sudan. As a result of the referendum, South Sudan separated from Sudan and established the South Sudan Republic. The PRC Government warmly congratulated the independence of South Sudan, announced its recognition of South Sudan Republic and established diplomatic relations with it on that very day it gained independence. As for the problems that remain unsolved between South Sudan and North Sudan, China believes they can be solved through negotiation and consultation. China hopes South Sudan and North Sudan become long lasting good neighbors, good partners and good brothers.

On the North Korean nuclear issue

The international security environment has undergone tremendous changes after the end of the Cold War. On the one hand, some countries started their efforts to develop nuclear weapons for their own security or other concerns. On the other hand, the proliferation of weapons of mass destruction and their delivery system has become a major worry of and a hot issue in the international community. The nuclear issues in North Korea and Iran are two salient examples.

The North Korean nuclear issue has remained a focus of international concern since its emergence in the early 1990s. As a close neighbor who has vital interests in the settlement of North Korean nuclear issue, China has paid close attention to the issue and has vigorously engaged in multilateral diplomacy in order to solve the North Korean nuclear issue. After the issue escalated in 2003, China hosted first the Three-Party Talks (China, North Korea and the United States) and then the Six-Party Talks (China, the Democratic Republic of Korea, the United States, the Republic of Korea, Russia and Japan) in Beijing. China has been instrumental in getting the participants to issue the *Initial Actions for*

the Implementation of the Joint Statement in February 2007 and *Second-Phase Actions for the Implementation of the Joint Statement* in October 2007, which have set the final goal of a nuclear-free Korean Peninsula.

As an opponent of nuclear proliferation, China has advocated for the denuclearization of the Korean Peninsula and has made relentless efforts to maintain long-lasting peace and stability in the Peninsula. After North Korea conducted two nuclear tests on October 9, 2006 and May 25, 2009, China joined other members of the Six-Party Talks to condemn the acts and voted for sanction measures targeting at the areas related to North Korea's nuclear and missile program in the UNSC. China again expressed its strong discontent and resolute opposition when the Korean side, in disregard of international opposition, conducted its third nuclear test in February 2013. Chinese Foreign Minister summoned North Korean Ambassador to Beijing to make a strong representation. He demanded that North Korea stop making any speech or taking any action

A plenary session of Six-Party Talks on North Korea's Nuclear Programme was held in Beijing.

that might further deteriorate the situation and return to the track of dialogue and consultation as soon as possible. In the UN, China supported the UNSC to pass Resolution 2094 which imposed sanction on North Korea and increased the intensity of carrying out the resolution.

China's position on North Korean nuclear issue is that the relevant parties should stick to the goal of denuclearizing the Korean Peninsula, stand firm in maintaining peace and stability on the Peninsula, and adhere to a settlement through dialogue and consultation no matter how the situation changes. At the same time China has held that the sovereignty, territorial integrity, and other legitimate security concerns, as well as its interests of development of DPRK, as a sovereignty and member of the United Nations, should be respected, and that the DPRK should enjoy the same rights of peaceful use of nuclear technology as other signatories once the DPRK returns to the *Non-proliferation Treaty*. It is China's consistent position that a negotiated solution through dialogue is the right way to solve the nuclear issue on the Peninsula, and the Six-Party Talks are an effective platform to promote denuclearization on the Korean Peninsula. China is in opposition to any action that may worsen the situation of peace and stability on the Korean Peninsula. China hopes the relevant parties can keep calm and exercise restraints once encountered new situation and resume the Six-Party Talks at an early date.

On Iran nuclear issue

The Iran nuclear issue, which is identical in nature with the North Korean issue, escalated into an international hot one in 2003. Iran has insisted that it is entitled to the rights of peaceful use of nuclear technology, but has had flip-flops in its cooperation with the International Atomic Energy Agency (IAEA) and with its suspension of uranium enrichment activities. The West has exerted pressures on Iran's nuclear plan, leading to a deadlock between Iran and the West over this issue.

In October 2013, the first round of the six-party talks on Iranian nuclear issues was held in Geneva after the new government of Iran taking office. Iran and the United States, Britain, France, Russia, China and Germany started a new round of negotiation on the nuclear issue.

China has been in favor of the international nuclear non-proliferation system. Since the Iranian nuclear crisis started, China has been working to promote a peaceful settlement through dialogue so as to uphold the international non-proliferation regime and peace as well as stability in the Middle East. China has been of the view that Iran should enjoy the rights of peaceful use of nuclear technology. China has appreciated Iranian policy that it did not have the plan to develop nuclear weapons and that it was willing to cooperate with the IAEA. China also held that Iran, a signatory of the *Non-Proliferation Treaty*, should live up to its international commitments, help maintain the liability of the international non-proliferation mechanism, and enhance its cooperation with the IAEA as it enjoys its rights of peaceful use of nuclear technology. China has been actively involved in the examining process over the Iranian nuclear issue in the IAEA and the United Nations Security Council, and China has participated in the conferences of the Foreign Ministers of Six Countries on Iran's nuclear issue and the political director-generals from the foreign ministries of the six countries, and has hosted the political director-generals from the foreign ministries of the six countries meeting on the Iranian nuclear issue in Shanghai in April 2008 in order to seek a peaceful settlement of the Iran nuclear issue.

After long diplomatic wrestling, a framework agreement on the settlement of Iran Nuclear issue was reached between Iran and the six countries of the U.S., Britain, Russia, France, China and Germany in November 2103, making an important step toward diplomatic settlement of the Iranian nuclear issue. As a party of the Six-Party talks, China has contributed constructively to the agreement. China hopes all the relevant parties to implement the agreement jointly and faithfully and to maintain the momentum of dialogue so as to move toward a long term and complete settlement of the Iranian nuclear issue at an early date in accordance with the principle of mutual respect, step by step and reciprocity.

The Syrian Issue

Political crisis took place in Syrian in March 2011 and soon developed to serious domestic strife, sinking the country into civil war. The turmoil has caused great suffering and trauma to both the Syrian people and Syria's neighbors and caught broad attention from the international community. The U.S. and Europe imposed sanctions on Syria, and the League of Arab States (LAS) exerted pressures on it. The Syrian Government bogged down into serious crisis.

From the beginning of the crisis, China advocated for starting at an early date an inclusive political process led by Syrians and participated extensively by all parties to seek a peaceful settlement of the conflict through dialogue and consultation and restore the situation to stability at the early date. Once the civil war broke out, China urged the Syrian government and other political parties stop all violent activities immediately and completely and immediately start inclusive

On December 31, 2013, a Chinese Navy vessel was leaving to escort Syrian chemical weapons en route to be destroyed in the Mediterranean. According to decision of OPCW on destruction of Syria's chemical weapons and the resolution 2118 adopted by the UN Security Council, the chemical weapons of Syria would be transited to the U.S. ships to be eliminated. China, Russia, Denmark and Norway sent warships to escort the ships loaded with the Syrian chemical weapons.

political dialogue without any precondition so as to work out a comprehensive plan and mechanism through negotiation.

China was in opposition to the settlement of the Syrian issue through force and was firmly against externally forced "regime change" and other actions that violated the goals and principles of the *UN Charter* and other fundamental international norms. China and Russia casted their veto on two draft resolutions on Syrian on October 4, 2011 and February 4, 2012 at the UNSC and voted down the draft resolutions on Syria tabled by some countries, avoiding domestic chaos and disasters resulted from external interference in the domestic affairs of the countries in this area from happening again.

China was distressed and deeply concerned about the affected people. China respected the wishes of Syrian people. China maintained contact with both the Syrian government and opposition parties to encourage dialogues and a peaceful solution, while continuing to provide humanitarian support.

At the same time, the Chinese government made positive and balanced efforts for the peaceful settlement of the Syrian issue. China dispatched its special envoys to visit Syria and other countries in the Middle East to engage in good office. China maintains contacts with all parties of the Syrian civil war, including the Syrian government, and major countries in the Middle East and put forward six proposals on the political settlement of the Syrian issue. China urged the Syrian government and relevant parties to end hostility and violence instantly and cooperate with the UN, the International Committee of the Red Cross and other organizations to alleviate the humanitarian situation. China called for relevant parties to enhance communication and make concerted efforts to work out a peaceful and proper settlement of the Syrian issue within the framework of the LAS on the basis of plans of political settlement proposed by the LAS.

China followed the humanitarian situation in Syria with great concern and has provided assistance within its capacity to the Syrian people, including Syrian refugees outside the country. The assistance include US$ 11 million humanitarian aid to civilians both in and outside Syria, emergency humanitarian material aid to Jordan worth RMB 15 million, and emergency humanitarian aid in cash worth RMB 24 million to the World Food Program and the World Health Organization for the displaced people within Syria and Syrian refugees in Lebanon respectively. However, China is in opposition to any actions of actual interference with Syria's internal affairs in the name of "humanitarian" issue.

In August 2013 chemical attacks took place in the east suburb of Damask Syria, which resulted in large casualties and shocked the world. The two parties of the civil war in Syria accused each other. Countries led by the U.S. alleged the Syrian government for responsibility and planned for military attacks and this was opposed by Russia. The U.S. and Russia reached a framework agreement in Geneva, which provided the Syrian authorities destroys all its chemical weapons by the mid of 2014 and join the *Convention on the Prohibition of Chemical Weapons* as the provincial settlement of the issue. The UNSC unanimously passed Resolution 2118 which confirmed the practice of "turning over control chemical weapons for peace." The resolution required Syria to cooperate with the Organization for the Prohibition of Chemical Weapons (OPCW) and the UN and destroy its chemical weapons plan.

China firmly opposed the use of chemical weapons by any country or any people and strongly condemned the use of chemical weapons in Syria. Meanwhile, China stood behind settlement of the Syrian chemical weapons and related issues through peaceful means and was in opposition to military intervention from the outside. China welcomed and endorsed Russia's proposal and voted for the UNSC Resolution 2118. China hoped to see the Security Council's resolution and the decision of the OPCW be carried out thoroughly and accurately and hoped that the UN and OPCW launch the verification and destruction of chemical weapons professionally in a objective, fair and neutral way. China expressed its readiness to send experts and make financial contribution for the destruction of chemical weapons in Syria.

China's Diplomacy Pattern

Mutual respect for sovereignty and territorial integrity, mutual non-aggression, non-interference in each other's internal affairs, equality and mutual benefit, and peaceful co-existence are important international norms. China's diplomacy has been characterized by developing peaceful and friendly relations with all countries on the basis of these five principles.

China has continuously adhered to the five principles of peaceful co-existence in its foreign relations and has energetically developed relations with different countries of the world. On the basis of the five principles of peaceful co-existence, China's relations with developed countries have maintained stability on the whole. Relations with its neighbors are the best since the founding of the PRC, and its solidarity and cooperative relations with developing countries have been further strengthened, making China's international and peripheral environment the best since 1949.

The Development of the Five Principles of Peaceful Co-existence

The Five Principles of Peaceful Co-existence was first proposed by Chinese then-Premier Zhou Enlai when meeting with an India delegation visiting China in December 1943 to negotiate with its Chinese counterpart on questions concerning their relations in the Tibet regions of China. Then-Premier Zhou Enlai proposed in his talks with the Indian delegation, "Immediately after its birth, New China has set its principles in handling its relations with India, namely: mutual respect for territorial integrity, mutual non-aggression, non-interference in each other's internal affairs, equality and mutual benefit, peaceful coexistence." The Indian side agreed with this view, and the five principles were included in the Preamble to the *Agreement between the People's Republic of China and the Republic of India on Trade and Intercourse Between the Tibet Region of China and India.*

In April 1995, Premier Zhou Enlai attended Asian-African Conference held in Bandung, Indonesia, and reiterated the Five Principles of Peaceful Coexistence of China.

The Chinese delegation led by Zhou Enlai participated in the Asian-African (Bandung) Conference participated by 29 countries from Asia and Africa, which was held in Bandung, Indonesia in April 1955. The 10 principles on international relations adopted in the final communiqué of the conference is an extension of the Five Principles of Peaceful Co-existence. Thereafter, China has settled the boundary issues that were left over from history with Burma, Mongolia, Pakistan, and Afghanistan consecutively on the basis of the Five Principles of Peaceful Co-existence.

In his tour to 14 countries in Asia, Africa, and Europe at the end of 1963 to early 1964, Zhou Enlai put forward eight principles for China's economic and technical aid to foreign countries, which extended the Five Principles of Peaceful Co-existence to the field of international economic cooperation. Many international instruments, including the "*Joint Communiqué between the People's Republic of China and the United States of America*" (also referred to as the "*Shanghai Communiqué*") reached between the two governments when American President Nixon visited China in 1972, the *Joint Communiqué on the Establishment of Diplomatic Relations between the People's Republic of China and the United States of America* in 1978, as well as the Sino-Japanese Treaty of Peace and Friendship signed by the two governments in 1978, have all emphasized the Five Principles of Peaceful Co-existence as the guiding principles in developing bilateral relations.

The five principles were put forward with initial emphasis for guiding China's relations with countries with different social systems. But late historical experiences have revealed that if the Five Principles of Peaceful Co-existence are adhered to, countries with different social systems can live in harmony and maintain amicable cooperation. Even countries with similar social systems may come into sharp confrontation or even conflicts. Whether relations between countries are good or bad depends on whether or not they strictly adhere to these principles.

Conference Marking the 60th Anniversary of the Five Principles of Peaceful Coexistence

2014年6月28日 北京
June 28, 2014 Beijing

In June 2014, a meeting to commemorate the 60th anniversary of the initiation of the Five Principles of Peaceful Coexistence was held in Beijing.

The Constitution of the PRC adopted by the fifth session of the fifth National People Congress provides, "China adheres to an independent foreign policy as well as to the five principles of mutual respect for sovereignty and territorial integrity, mutual non-aggression, non-interference in each other's internal affairs, equality and mutual benefit, and peaceful co-existence in developing diplomatic relations and economic and cultural exchanges with other countries."

China is not only an advocator but a practitioner of the Five Principles of Peaceful Co-existence. So far the Five Principles of Peaceful Co-existence have been written in the communiqués or other important bilateral instruments between China and 172 countries that have diplomatic relations with China. China sticks to the Five Principles of Peaceful Co-existence in establishing and developing relations with all countries of the world, and has formed a good foreign relations structure. On the international stage, China proposes to build a peaceful, stable, fair, and reasonable international political order and international economic order based on the Five Principles of Peaceful Co-existence.

Maintaining Stable and Peaceful Relations with Developed Countries

Diplomacy is an important instrument for countries to further their foreign policy goals and to safeguard their national interests. National interests are multi-dimensional and have special emphasis under different environments in different times. In the first 30 years after the founding of the PRC, the priority of China's national interests was to safeguard national sovereignty, territorial integrity and security. With the shift from political to economic issues domestically, the priority of China's national interests since the 1980s have changed to that of promoting China's economic development, unremittingly increasing China's comprehensive national strength, and improving the living standard and quality of the Chinese people. Consequently, the major task of China's diplomacy changed to creating an international environment of lasting peace and a favorable climate in China's periphery for domestic economic construction.

In light of China's current foreign-policy goal, it is of special significance to maintain a stable relationship with developed countries of the world. From the perspective of keeping China's economic development, major developed countries, namely, the United States, European Union and Japan, are China's major trade partners. According to Chinese statistics, China's trade with the three major economies accounted for more than 40 percent of China's total trade volume in the last few years, and their investment in China amounted to a quarter of China's total foreign investment. In addition, they are also the major sources of Chinese high-tech import and the major target countries of Chinese students who go abroad for further studies. A stable relationship with developed countries has been one of the main experiences of China's foreign policy successes after its opening-up and reform, and also a precondition for China to continue its sustained economic development domestically.

From a political and security perspective, China has a political system, value and living style that are different from those of the developed countries, and many of the political, security problems that China faces today more or less have something to do with them. Moreover, the bilateral relations between China and these countries could impact China's relations with other countries, and in the long run will affect whether China will be able to reach its diplomatic goal. For this reason the Political Report to the 18th Party Congress points out that China will improve and grow our relations with developed countries by expanding areas of cooperation and properly addressing differences with them. China will strive to establish a new type of relations of long-term stability and sound growth with other major countries.

Maintaining stable and healthy Sino-American relations

China's relations with the United States have been the key of the keys among China's relations with all the western big powers. China is the biggest developing country, and the U.S. the biggest developed country. Therefore Sino-US relations are important not only for the two countries but for the world as a whole. Having experienced 60 years of difficulties and hardships, including confrontations and frictions as well as cooperation and coordination, the two sides have formed a highly interdependent relationship through enhancing communications and deepening exchanges.

In retrospect, the 60 years of Sino-US relations can be divided into three 20-year periods. The first 20 years after New China's founding witnessed a Sino-US rivalry, confrontation, and conflicts. The U.S. refused to recognize the government of the PRC, and pursued a China policy of political isolation, economic embargo, and military containment. To safeguard its hard-won sovereignty, independence, and territorial integrity, the New Chinese government had to engage in battles and struggles with the U.S.

The second 20 years was a period of Sino-US strategic cooperation. The changing balance of power between the U.S. and the Soviet Union in the late 1960s not only changed international structure but helped bring about the Sino-US rapprochement. China and the U.S. released the *Shanghai Communiqué* during President Nixon's visit to China in 1972, which not only opened the door for Sino-US diplomatic normalization but also started the process of bilateral strategic cooperation. The realization of bilateral diplomatic relations in 1979 landed China and the U.S. on a new stage and ushered in a brand new period of cooperation in strategic, economic and trade, education and cultural areas.

Sino-US relations entered their third 20 years of turmoil, adjustment and breaking after the end of the Cold War. The turmoil started when the U.S.

In 1972 Mao Zedong met with President Nixon during his visit to China.

imposed sanctions on China in 1989. The U.S. government, disregarding its commitments on reducing arms sales to Taiwan, made a decision to sell Taiwan fighter planes worth $6 billion in 1992. It again contradicted itself by allowing Lee Teng-hui, Taiwan leader and an advocator of "Taiwan independence" to visit the U.S. in 1995. The U.S.-led NATO, while intervening in the internal affairs of former Yugoslavia, bombed the Chinese Embassy in Yugoslavia in 1999. In 2001, the U.S. government increased its air surveillance on China leading to a collision between an American spy plane and a Chinese fighter plane near Chinese territory, resulting in the destruction of the Chinese plane and the death of its pilot. All these infringe upon Chinese sovereignty by the U.S. caused strong opposition and protest from Chinese people and the Chinese government, and Sino-US relations suffered repeated setbacks.

Differences do remain between China and the U.S. under the current situation. However, their common interests have been on the rise and by far surpass their differences. China and the U.S. share common interests on a large array issues, including maintaining world peace; settling global and regional issues, such as on the prevention of weapons of mass destruction; settling the nuclear issue in Korean Peninsula and Iran; cracking down on transnational crimes; coping with climate change and natural disaster relief; and controlling the spread of infectious diseases. Enhancing communication and cooperation over these issues has become the new basis of bilateral strategic cooperation.

Fast-growing economic and trade relations have become a new catalyst for the development of bilateral relations. The volume of bilateral trade, which was $2.4 billion in 1979 when the Sino-US diplomatic relations were normalized, has surpassed US$ 500 billion and mutual investment was more than US$ 100 billion in 2012. The two countries are now each other's second largest trading partner and such relations have brought huge benefits to each country's development. They have served as a stabilizer that enables China-US relations to forge ahead despite winds and waves.

In January 1979, Deng Xiaoping made a visit to the United States and attended the welcome ceremony held by President Carter in the White House. This was the first time for the Chinese leaders to visit the U.S.

In addition to economic and trade cooperation, high-level contacts and exchanges between China and the United States at different levels are getting ever-more frequent, and the two countries have established more than 90 dialogue and consultation mechanisms in six major categories, covering political relations, economy, military-to-military relations, law enforcement, science and technology, education, energy, environmental protection, aviation and so on and so forth.

Moreover, the bilateral relations are no longer restricted to the relationship between the two states or the two governments. Rather they have expanded to bilateral relations between two societies and two peoples. For instance, people-to-people exchanges, which were scarce when the bilateral relations were first normalized, reached 4 million person/times every year with more than 10 thousands people flowing between the two sides of the Pacific Ocean.

China has 235,000 students studying in the U.S. and is the largest sources of foreign students in the U.S. During his visit to China in 2009 President Obama announced the "100,000 Strong" Initiative in order to send 100,000 students to come study in China. So far the program has supported 68,000 American students studying in China. In 35 year after bilateral normalization, the two sides have 41 sister provinces/states and 201 sister cities. All these have jointly bound China and the U.S. together.

Differences and frictions increase as the bilateral ties were enhanced, and Taiwan remains the most sensitive and crucial issue among all the differences between China and the U.S. In spite of China's consistent opposition, the U.S. has insisted on selling weapons to Taiwan, and upgraded its substantial relations with Taiwan. These all encroached upon China's sovereignty, interfered with

In July 2013, the 5th round of the U.S.-China Strategic and Economic Dialogue was held in Washington.

China's internal affairs, and undermined China's core national interests. Besides, the U.S. has often made use of the Tibet, human rights, religion, and other issues that are purely China's domestic in nature to interfere in China's internal affairs. Such U.S. policies are detrimental to the overall Sino-US cooperation and are strongly opposed by the Chinese government.

China sets great store by Sino-US relations and hopes that the bilateral relations could develop stably and smoothly on the principles enshrined in the three bilateral joint communiqués. The two countries reached a consensus on making a joint effort to build constructive and cooperative China-US relations during the first meeting between Chinese President Hu Jintao and American President Barack Obama when they participated in the G20 financial summit held in London in Aril 2009. To implement the consensus, the two sides have launched a mechanism of Sino-American Strategic and Economic Dialogues, which has become an important platform for the two sides to expand consensus, reduce differences, deepen mutual trust, and promote cooperation.

China-US Strategic and Economic Dialogue

Sino-US Strategic and Economic Dialogue is an overall dialogue between China and the U.S. over strategic, long-term issues of common concern in Sino-U.S. relations to meet the demand of deepening Sino-US relations against the background of globalization. It was launched in accordance with the agreement reached between the top leaders of the two countries. It is the highest-level and most abundant bilateral dialogue among the many mechanisms between the two countries. The first dialogue was held in Washington D.C. in July 2009. The second round was held in Beijing in May 2010. The third round was held in Washington D.C. in May 2011 and the Chinese Military participated in the dialogue for the first time. The fourth round was held in May 2012 in Beijing. The Fifth round was held in July

2013 in Washington D.C. During the dialogues the two sides hold in-depth discussions to sort out their common interests, promote Sino-U.S. relation in the new age, properly handle the differences and sensitive issues in the bilateral relations, enhance coordination over important global and regional issues, and deepen their cooperation in international system and Asia-Pacific affairs.

China and the United States are parts of a community of shared interests. Neither of us will benefit from confrontation. War will get us nowhere. How to manage Sino-U.S. relations is of great significance not only for the two countries but for the world at large. However, as the balance of power between China and the U.S. changes, the old logic of emerging power and status quo power engaging confrontation and war are like cloud hanging over Sino-U.S. relations, affecting the development of the bilateral relations.

In June 2013, President Xi Jinping held a historic meeting with American President Obama in Annenberg Estate, California at the latter's invitation. Xi Jinping proposed during their meeting a new model of major-country relations featuring "no conflict or confrontation", "mutual respect", and "win-win cooperation". The concept of a new model of major-country relations was to change the negative expectation, reduce mutual strategic mistrust, and prop up positive confidence for the bilateral, and charter the future course for the bilateral relations.

The path to build new model of major power relations between China and the U.S. should start from the Asia Pacific area and whether it will succeed or not will to a large extend also be determined in this area. The Asia Pacific region is an area where China and the U.S. interests are most intertwined and where the two sides most frequently interacted with each other. The two countries' policies in this area and their interaction have great significance on the development and stability in this area. As President Xi Jinping aptly pointed out, "The vast Pacific Ocean is broad enough to accommodate our two big countries." China respects the traditional influence and immediate interests of the United States in the Asia-Pacific and does not have the idea to push the U.S. out of the region. Rather, it hopes the United States will play a positive and constructive role in safeguarding peace, stability and development in the Asia-Pacific. China expects the United States will also respect China's interests and concerns in Asia-Pacific, which has been the home and root of the Chinese nation for thousands of years.

Deepening Sino-EU relations

China is the biggest developing country, while Europe is an area that has the most developed countries. European Union (EU) is the biggest economic group made up of developed countries. Sino-EU relations are one of the most important bilateral relations for China, and China's consistent policy has been to develop close relations with EU.

Constrained by the Cold War, France was the only Western European country that had established diplomatic relations with China by 1964. The rest of Europe began to have diplomatic relations with China in the 1970s as the international situation relaxed, and China established formal ties with EU (called European Community at that time) in 1975. So far China maintains diplomatic relations with all European countries but the Vatican.

With its foreign policy adjusted in the early 1980s, China has advanced a policy of developing relations with other countries regardless of their political system or ideology, which opened a new prospect for its relations with Western Europe, Canada, Australia, New Zealand, who are complementary in economic fields but with different political systems from China. Exchanges of high-level visits started, and trade volume increased quickly with various forms of cooperation in different fields. Under such favorable conditions, China reached agreements with Great Britain and Portugal respectively on the principles

In January 1964, France established the diplomatic relations with China, becoming the first western power setting up the diplomatic ties with the People's Republic of China. The picture is the group photo of Huang Zhen, China's first ambassador to France and President Charles de Gaulle after presenting his credential to French President.

concerning China's resumption of exercising sovereignty over Hong Kong and Macau.

Sino-EU relations experienced a setback in 1989 but returned to normal not long after. British Prime Minister and Italian Prime Minister paid consecutive visits to China in 1991, while Chinese President Jiang Zemin paid an official state visit to France in 1994, during which he put forward China's principles on developing relations with countries in Western Europe. And in the same year, the EU lifted all but arms embargoes on China that were imposed in 1989. Rapid progresses have been made ever since. In 1998 China and EU agreed to establish a mechanism of annual summits. In 2001, the two sides agreed to establish a comprehensive partnership, which was promoted to the comprehensive strategic partnership in 2003. The China-EU Annual Summit, established in 1998, is the highest level mechanism of political dialogue between the two sides and it has held 16 times by 2013. China and EU have established more than 60 mechanisms of consultation and dialogue covering political, economic and trade, humanitarian and social science, science and technology, energy, environmental and other fields.

Sino-EU relations are of global strategic significance from their beginning. China has always regarded very highly the role and influence of the EU in regional and international affairs, and welcomed the EU to play a constructive role in international affairs. China always supports European integration whether China's foreign policy theme was to maintain world peace and oppose hegemonism in the early days or promote multipolarization or democratization of international politics. *China's EU Policy Paper* issued by the Chinese Government in October 2003 elaborates EU's position in China's overall foreign relations, manifested China's determination in promoting Sino-EU relations to a long-term stable and comprehensive partnership. The document also puts forward China's EU policy goals, and details China's concrete ideas on strengthening Sino-EU relations in the field of politics, economic, education, science, culture, social, legal, administration, and the military.

The EU also attaches great importance to its relations with China and welcomes China's opening-up and development. It supports China to continue on its road of peaceful development. EU passed *A Long Term Policy EU-China Relations* in 1995 defining the strategic framework of EU China's policy. Since then the EU has consecutively issued the following policy papers to elaborate the guidelines, goals and principles in EU China policy: "EU's New Strategy in Cooperation with China" (1996), "Building a Comprehensive Partnership with China" (1998), "EU's China Strategy: the Implementation of 1998 Document and More Effective Steps to Promote EU's Policy in the Future" (2001), "A Maturating Partnership: Common Interest and Challenges for EU and China" (2003). In October 2006, EU published the sixth China policy paper since 1995.

In November 2013, Li Keqiang, Premier of the State Council of China, met pressmen together with Herman Van Rompuy, President of the European Council, and José Manuel Barroso, President of the European Commission, in Beijing to introduce the results of the 16th China-EU Summit.

Sound Sino-EU political relations have paved the way for bilateral economic relations. EU became China's largest trade partner in 2004, when the EU expanded eastward. The two-way trade reached US$ 546.04 billion in 2012 and EU has invested 36,639 projects in China with a total investment of US$ 83.93 billion, including 1698 projects with actual investment of US$ 6.11 billion in 2012, making EU China's biggest trade partner, largest exporting market and largest sources of technical import, and the fourth largest source of foreign investment. Almost all the big enterprises in the EU have investments in China. In the year 2012, China's non-financial investment in EU reached US$ 3.41 billion. As an important platform for Sino-EU communication in grand strategic issues, Sino-EU High Level Strategic Dialogue has been held for three rounds so far.

The progress in Sino-EU relations by no means implies that the bilateral relations have not encountered any difficulties. Among all the differences and difficulties that have the greatest harm to the bilateral relations are those that concern China's territorial and sovereignty integrity. For instance, the Netherlands government's insistence on selling Taiwan submarines in 1982, disregarding the Chinese government's strong opposition, led to the degrading of Sino-Dutch relations. The French government's decision to sell Taiwan Mirage-2000 fighters in 1992 caused a major setback in bilateral relations. Recent examples include some leaders from EU member countries French leader's insistence on meeting with Dalai Lama, who intends to separate Tibet from Chinese territory, not only leading to twists in China's relations with these countries but impacting China-EU relations as a whole. Furthermore, as the bilateral relations deepen, economic frictions become common occurrences in bilateral relations.

The EU Anti-dumping case against China's Solar Panel

Sino-EU economic and trade relations complement each other and have great potential. However as the bilateral trade grew, trade frictions became normal phenomena in bilateral relations. EU's anti-dumping cases against Chinese export to EU are most typical and one example is the anti-dumping investigation into Chinese export of solar panels announced by European Commission on September 6, 2012. The case would affect 21 billion euros (US$ 27.1 billion) worth of Chinese export to EU and was known as the biggest anti-dumping and anti-subsidy case the European Commission has launched in term of import value in its history.

The Chinese Government opposed trade protectionism and abuses of trade relief measures and considered them in no one's interest. Facing with the threat of sanctions, the Chinese Government stood firm in defending the interest of the solar profession and Chinese solar panel producers and initiated the process of anti-dumping and anti-subsidy complaint against EU export of wine to China. At the same time, the Chinese Government expressed desires to settle the dispute through dialogue and consultation so as to maintain the stable development of bilateral trade relations. Premier Li Keqiang reiterated China's stance over telephone talk with European Commission President Jose Manuel Barroso. He exchanged views with the German leader during his visit to Germany, and the two sides agreed to solve this issue through negotiation. The Chinese Ministry of Commerce dispatched a delegation to Germany, France and EU for negotiation.

After more than ten month's hard negotiation, China and EU reached a price commitment agreement on July 27, 013. The Chinese side committed to set a minimum price for solar panel export to EU and set certain ceiling for China solar panel export to EU. In return, the EU side committed to withdraw the anti-dumping measures against Chinese solar panel products. The agreement testified that negotiation is the most effectual means to defuse problems arising in China and EU cooperation so as to avoid trade frictions, expand their trade scales and reach mutual benefit and win-win result.

As political relation enhanced and economic and trade relations grew, Sino-EU People-to-people and cultural exchanges are also expanding. As of the end of 2012, China has established 105 Confucius Institutes in 25 EU member countries and 107 Confucius Classrooms in 13 EU member countries. The total number of Chinese students studying in EU reached 242,900. 35,400 students from 27 EU member countries are studying in China, accounting for 10.8% of foreign students coming to study in China in 2012.

However, China and EU do not have conflict in their respective interests, nor does the comprehensive partnership demand that the two sides should agree on every issue. What is needed is that the two sides reduce differences, enlarge mutual trust, and broaden the scope of their cooperation on the basis of seeking common ground while reserving differences. China on its part is in a position to respect each other's core interest along with EU and continuously substantiate and develop comprehensive strategic partnerships with EU on the basis of the Five Principles of Peaceful Co-existence.

Developing friendly relations with Japan for generations to come

Japan and China are neighboring countries with a long history of traditional friendship, separated only by a strip of water. Japanese militarism waged wars against China before the founding of the PRC and caused great sufferings for the Chinese people. The late Chinese Premier Zhou Enlai used to refer the unpleasant history as saying "(The Sino-Japanese relations are) 2,000 years of friendship, and 50 years of confrontation," and he put forward the principles for developing the bilateral relations: "learning from history and facing up to the future."

In September 1972, Chinese and Japanese governments issued a joint statement in Beijing for the normalization of bilateral relations. The picture is Premier Zhou Enlai and Kakuei Tanaka, Prime Minister of Japan, exchanging the signed copies of Sino-Japanese Joint Statement.

In August 1978, the Treaty of Peace and Friendship between Japan and the People's Republic of China was signed in Beijing.

Thanks to the shifts with the international structure in the 1970s, China and Japan put an end to the abnormal state of affairs that existed between the two countries and established diplomatic ties in 1972. According to the provisions of the *Sino-Japanese Joint Statement* for normalizing bilateral relations, the two sides negotiated and signed *Sino-Japanese Treaty of Peace and Friendship* in 1978, committing to develop bilateral relations on the basis of the Five Principles of Peaceful Co-existence, which laid the political foundation for the good-neighborly relationship between China and Japan.

Great progress has been achieved in Sino-Japanese relations since the 1980s. Exchanges of high level visits have been frequent, and bilateral cooperative mechanisms at different levels have been established, such as the Joint Cabinet Member Conferences, the Sino-Japanese Friendship Committee of 21st Century formed by senior, junior, and young generation members from the two sides, the Regulatory Consultations between the Two Foreign Ministers, and Sino-Japanese Security Consultation.

Sound development of political relations has created a favorable environment for Sino-Japanese cooperation in economic, trade, and other areas. The Chinese government declared in the *Sino-Japanese Joint Statement* that "in the interest of the friendship between the Chinese and the Japanese peoples, it (China) renounces its demand for war reparation from Japan." On the Japanese side, it has provided four packages of government yen loans to China amounting to Japanese yen 2.65 trillion from 1979 to 2000. Bilateral trade reached US$ 329.4 billion in 2012. The high-growth rate of the Chinese economy has brought about important opportunities for Japan, making China an important external driving force for Japan's economy to recover from the low ebb to the track of sustained growth. Due to the stagnation of Japanese economy and the cold bilateral political relations, Japan has dropped from China's number 3 trade partner in 2010 to number 5 in 2013.

Disaccorded notes remain in the main melody of peaceful and friendly Sino-Japanese relations. The biggest disturbance concerns how the Japanese government treats its history of aggression. In the *Joint Statement* that marked the normalization of the bilateral relations, the Japanese side admitted that it "is keenly conscious of the responsibility for the serious damage that Japan caused in the past to the Chinese people through war, and deeply reproaches itself." However, since the 1980s, the Japanese government has "examined and approved" some high school history textbooks that distorted and beautified the history of aggression, and has caused protests from China and Japan's other Asian neighbors. In 1985, the Japanese Prime Minister paid homage in his official capacity to the Yasukuni Shrine where 14 class A World War II criminals were worshiped. This was protested by China and other Asian countries, and since then, the Japanese leaders have stopped paying homage to the shrine. But by the beginning of the 21st century, the Japanese leader disregarded the opposition from Chinese and other Asian peoples, and insisted on visiting the shrine in the name of prime minister, leading to the suspension of high-level visits between China and Japan, a situation referred to as Sino-Japanese "Political Cold and Economic

Hot." Such situation not only undermined Japan's relations with China and its other Asian neighbors but destabilized regional stability and hindered the East Asia integration process.

The Yasukuni Shrine Issue

Japanese invaded some of its neighbors in history and has brought serious calamities and sufferings to these countries. How the Japanese Government treats its invasion in history is a very sensitive political issue in Japan's relations with its Asian neighbors including China. The Yasukuni Shrine issue is the touchstone of this issue.

Yasukuni Shrine is a Shinto shrine located in Tokyo, Japan, where the Japanese soldiers and their relatives who died in wars since the Meiji time were honored. It was the spiritual pillar of Japanese military aggression before WWII. In 1978, the names of 14 class-A criminals from World War II War criminals prosecuted by the International Military Tribunal for the Far East were included and honored in the enshrinement in addition to 2000 Class-C and Class-D crime. It is regarded as a symbol of Japanese militarism by many countries.

An official visit by Prime Minister Yasuhiro Nakasone on August 15, 1985 was strongly criticized by its neighbors in Asia and led to a diplomatic crisis. Neither he nor his several successors visited the shrine again in order not to provoke its neighbors. Junichiro Koizumi, in disregard of strong opposition from China and South Korea, insisted visiting the Shrine after he becomes Japanese Prime Minister in 2001, leading Sino-Japanese relations to freeze. Prime Minister Shinzo Abe visited the shrine on December 26, 2013 after seven years in which no sitting prime minister had visited the Shrine, worsened the bilateral relations which had plagued by the

Diaoyu Dao Islands Issue. The Chinese Government lodged solemn representations, strongly protested and severely condemned against the Japanese side.

In the eyes of China and other Asian countries, Japanese leaders' visit to the Yasukuni Shrine is by no means a domestic affair of Japan, still less an act by an individual. It in essence boils down to whether or not Japan is able to correctly look at and profoundly repent its past of militarist aggression and colonial rule. It is a matter of major principle that bears on the political foundation of Japan's relations with its Asian neighbors including China and the international community. It is a serious political and diplomatic issue.

The Taiwan issue is another factor hindering Sino-Japanese relations. Japan had a 50-year-long colonial rule over Taiwan, which was returned to China according to the relevant international instruments. The *Sino-Japanese Joint Statement* provides: "The government of the People's Republic of China reiterates that Taiwan is an inalienable part of the territory of the People's Republic of China. The government of Japan fully understands and respects this stand of the government of the People's Republic of China, and it firmly maintains its stand under Article 8 of the *Potsdam Proclamation*." However illusions never ceased to exist among some Japanese politicians who keep the intention to interfere with the Taiwan issue. China has made its policy unambiguously that it does not oppose Japan having non-official relations with Taiwan, but it is strongly against Japan having any official relations with Taiwan that would lead to "two Chinas" or "One China, One Taiwan" in whatever forms. This principle has been reemphasized in other important instruments in Sino-Japanese relations.

Considering the concerns from Chinese and people of other countries that were invaded by Japan, the new Japanese leaders stopped paying homage

The Chinese maritime police patrol ships are cruising around Diaoyu Island.

to the Yasukuni Shrine in October 2006, removing the major obstacle in the development of Sino-Japanese relations. After a period of "freeze" in Sino-Japanese relations, Prime Minister Shinzo Abe paid an official visit to China, which was called "ice-breaking visit" in 2006. In April 2007, Chinese Premier Wen Jiabao returned a "ice-melting visit" to Japan, during which the two parties issued a *Sino-Japanese Joint Communiqué* that reaffirmed the two sides' efforts to develop a bilateral "strategic relationship of mutual benefit," putting the bilateral relations on the normal track. Japanese Prime Minister Yasuo Fukuda's "meeting the spring visit" to China in May 2008 and Chinese President Hu Jintao's "warm spring visit" to Japan demonstrated that Sino-Japanese relations are now on a normal track.

In September 2012, the Japanese Government, in disregard of Chinese side's opposition and going against the consensus on "leaving the issue of Diaoyu Islands to be resolved later" the two sides reached when their bilateral relations were normalized in 1972 and the acquiesce of "shelving the disputes and leaving the issue to be resolved later" reached when the two sides signed the Sino-Japanese Treaty of Peace and Friendship in 1978, decided to "nationalize the Diaoyu Islands. " The Japanese side's action changed the status quo, leading Sino-Japanese relations to a most difficult situation since their normalization. As a result, the attitude of the two peoples toward each other dropped to a historical low and bilateral relation sank into its lowest ebb.

The Chinese Government's position is that Diaoyu Islands and its affiliated islands have been an inherent territory of China since ancient times. China enjoys historical and legal foundations for such position. Whatever means the Japanese side takes unilaterally on the Diaoyu Islands is illegal, ineffective and futile. It will not change the fact that the Diaoyu Islands belong to China. The Chinese side presses Japan to respect history, face the reality squarely and engage in serious negotiation with China over the nature of the Diaoyu Islands so as to find a means to manage the disputes and get the problem solved.

China and Japan are respectively the world's number 2 and number 3 economies. The volume of their economy accounts for 20% of that of East Asia and 80% of that of the world. They shoulder important responsibilities for the stability, development and prosperity of the region. Good Sino-Japanese relations are good fortune for the two people, and bad Sino-Japanese relations are misfortune for the two peoples. China considers Japan an important, peaceful, mutual beneficial partner that could achieve win-win results with China. China is ready to develop Sino-Japanese relations of peaceful co-existence and mutual benefit, attaining common development for generations to come in accordance with the principles enshrined in the *Sino-Japanese Joint Declaration* and other political documents.

Strengthening Good Neighborly Relations

With respect to geography, the environment and intertwined relations, the neighboring region has major strategic significance for China. In reviewing the experiences of its relations with neighboring countries, China is determined to develop a good neighborly relation and make relations with its neighbors as the priority of China's diplomacy. China's current policy is to forge a more peaceful, stable, developing and prosperous peripheral environment.

Many of China's neighbors got independence from western colonial rule at around the time the PRC was founded, marking a new starting point for China's relations with its neighbors. The first generation leadership of the CPC Central Committee with Mao Zedong as the core led a resolute struggle against big

In 1960, China and Burma signed the treaties and agreements on the border issues in Beijing. This is the first time for New China to officially settle the border issues left over from history with neighboring countries.

In December 2012, the 11th meeting of premiers of the SCO state members was held in Bishkek, capital of Kyrgyzstan.

power's political isolation, military "containment" and economic sanction on China from neighboring areas and safeguarded China's territorial and sovereignty integrity. While settling the issues left over from history with India, China put forward the Five Principles of Peaceful Co-existence, and jointly proposed to the world these principles with India and Burma. Based on the principle of equality and mutual benefit, China has settled boundary issues left over from history consecutively with Burma, Nepal, Afghanistan, Mongolia, and Korea, making most parts of China's borders friendly and peaceful.

After China's opening-up, the second generation of CPC Central Committee's collective leadership with Deng Xiaping as the nucleus made adjustment to China's domestic and foreign policy according to situational changes. While switching the focus of domestic work, it highlighted that the main task of diplomatic work is to create a sound international environment especially peripheral environment for China's domestic economic construction.

China actively developed good neighborly relations with peripheral countries, consolidated relations with traditional friendly countries, gradually improved relations with Mongolia, Vietnam, India and other neighbors.

After the end of the Cold War, the third generation of leadership with Jiang Zemin as the core put forward a new concept of security with "mutual trust, mutual benefits, equality and coordination" as the core and established the Shanghai Cooperative Organization along with Russia, Kazakhstan, Kyrgyzstan, and Tajikistan in 2001. While addressing the Southeast Asia's financial crisis in 1997, 10+1 (Ten ASEAN countries plus China) and 10+3 (Ten ASEAN countries plus China, Japan and South Korea) were formed. From 1996, China has reached agreement with India, Pakistan, Nepel, and ASEAN consecutively to form a partnership of different kind.

In August 2013, the special meeting of Foreign Ministers for the 10th anniversary of establishment of the strategic partnership between China and ASEAN was held in Beijing.

From the beginning of the new century, the CPC Central Committee with Hu Jintao as the Secretary General set store by peripheral diplomacy and put forward the idea of "secure, good, rich neighbor" and promoted friendship and partnership with neighbors. China has forcefully promoted economic and trade relations with ASEAN through the framework of 10+3 and 10+1, spearheaded the Six-party talk on the Korean Peninsula's nuclear issue. The good neighborly relation and pragmatic cooperation between China and its neighbors has created a peaceful stable, equal and mutual trust, cooperation and win-win peripheral environment making China's relations with its neighbors the best in history.

The Political Report to the 18th CPC National Congress points out, China will continue to promote friendship and partnership with its neighbors, consolidate friendly relations and deepen mutually beneficial cooperation with them, and ensure that China's development will bring more benefits to its neighbors. The CPC Central Committee with Xi Jinping as the Secretary General upgraded good diplomatic work in neighboring countries to a new level and considered it the necessity to realize the "two centenary goals" and realize the Chinese dream of a great national rejuvenation.

China's development provides an opportunity for its neighbors and China also benefit from it. During this process, the interactive exchanges and integration of interest between China and Asia as well as the world are both unprecedented in both scope and depth. The trade volume between China and its neighbors has increased from US$ 100 billion to US$ 1.3 trillion in the new century. China has become the biggest trade partner, the largest export market and important sources of foreign investment for many neighboring countries.

In less than one year after the new government was established, China has exchanged visits at the level of head of state or head of government with 21 neighboring countries, which have deepened the sentiment between China and its neighboring countries and facilitated cooperation. In October 2013, the Central Committee held the first ever conference on the diplomatic work on neighboring countries since the founding of the PRC, which laid out China's strategic goal, fundamental policy and overall pattern of China's neighboring diplomacy. The Conference underscored the concept of intimacy, sincerity, mutual benefit, and tolerance in developing relations with neighbors. Whether China can live together with its neighbor in harmony and give mutual help and protection will greatly condition the future of China's relations with the world.

The progress and steady development in its relations with Russia, China's biggest neighbor, is a model of China's successful good-neighborly relations. Sino-Russian relations developed from Sino-Soviet relations. The Soviet Union was the first country that recognized the PRC and the first country that established diplomatic ties with the PRC upon its founding, and Sino-Soviet relations witnessed a twist process of friendly allies in the 1950s, deterioration and confrontation in the 1960s and 1970s, and rapprochement and normalization in the 1980s.

The Soviet Union disintegrated on December 26, 1991, not long after the normalization of Sino-Soviet relations in 1989. As Russia inherited the legal status of the Soviet Union on the international stage, Sino-Soviet relations transitioned smoothly to peaceful Sino-Russian relations. The two sides agreed in December 1992 to deepen their bilateral relations on the basis of the *UN Charter*, the Five Principles of Peaceful Co-existence, and other recognized principles of international laws. The leaders of the two countries frequently exchange views on international or regional issues of common concern in their regular visits to each other's countries, in the UN and at the Shanghai Cooperative Organization (Shanghai Five) summits, promoting their bilateral relations from "constructive partnership" to "constructive strategic partnership" and finally to "partnership of strategic coordination based on equality and benefit and oriented towards the 21st century." The two heads of state signed in 2001 the *Treaty of Good Neighborliness and Friendly Cooperation between the People's Republic of China and the Russian Federation*, which laid a solid political foundation for stable bilateral relations. With unremitting efforts from both sides, the two countries have established comprehensive strategic partnership relations between them. Sino-Russian trade volume reached US$ 88.2 billion and people to people exchanges reached 3.3 million in 2102, bringing concrete benefits for the two peoples and demonstrating the great potential and prospect for Sino-Russian relations.

President Xi made Russia the first leg of his first overseas visit as China's President and he reached agreement with President Putin to cement Sino-Russia strategic and cooperative relations in all directions. The two sides reiterated their strong support for each other's development and rejuvenation, support for each other to safeguard their core interest, and support for each other to independently choose their road of development and social and political system. In less than one year after their first meeting, President Xi and President Putin have had meetings on five different international multilateral occasions, forging an intimate working relations and personal friendship between them. Through frequent high level meeting as such, China and Russia have further enhanced their strategic trust, upgraded practical cooperation, revitalize people-to-people exchange, strengthened international coordination, making China-Russia strategic partnership the highest level, with most solid foundation, most rich in content one with biggest regional and global influence in among China's partnership.

Sino-Russian Treaty of Friendship

The *Sino-Russian Treaty of Friendship*, signed by the two presidents in July 16, 2001, is a programmatic document for Sino-Russian relations in the new century. In light of historical experience, the treaty defined in the terms of law the peaceful concept "to develop the friendship between the people of the two countries from generation to generation" and the firm will to be everlasting good neighbors, good friends and goo partner. The treaty provides that they will neither resort to the use of force or the threat of force nor take economic and other means to bring pressure to bear against the other. The contracting parties will only solve their differences through peaceful means. The contracting parties reaffirm their commitment that they will not be the first to use nuclear weapons against each other nor target strategic nuclear missiles against each other. The two parties will adhere to the principles of non-encroachment upon territories and national boundaries as stipulated in international laws and build the border between the two countries into one where ever-lasting peace and friendship prevail. The treaty also provides that "When a situation arises in which one of the contracting parties deems that peace is being threatened and undermined or its security interests are involved or when it is confronted with the threat of aggression, the contracting parties shall immediately hold contacts and consultations in order to eliminate such threats." This treaty makes the strategic cooperative partnership of equality and mutual trust the model of Sino-Russian relations and its practical importance remains today.

China's policy to create a secure, amicable, and prosperous neighborhood had has an all dimensional feature. It is first manifested in its relations with Southeast countries. The Chinese government's policy during the Asian financial crisis in 1997 and its attitudes toward the remaining boundary disputes with certain countries changed the perception of Southeast countries toward China. In the political realm, China has enhanced mutual trust with ASEAN members by actively participating in the ASEAN Regional Forum (ARF), and has reached agreements of concrete substance through multilateral dialogue and cooperation, including the *Declaration on the Conduct of Parties in the South China Sea,* the *Joint Declaration of ASEAN and China on Cooperation in the Field of Non-*

In May 2014, President Xi Jinping held a welcome ceremony in Shanghai to welcome President Vladimir Putin to visit China.

Traditional Security Issues, and the *Treaty of Amity and Cooperation in Southeast Asia* in 2003.

In the economic realm, the bilateral trade and economic relations between China and ASEAN members have been forcefully strengthened through the cooperative framework of ASEAN and China, Japan and South Korea (10+3), and ASEAN and China (10+1). China and ASEAN have signed the *Framework Agreement on Comprehensive Economic Co-Operation* in 2002 and the two sides agreed to establish a strategic partnership in 2003. China-ASEAN relations entered a "golden decade" after China becomes the first non-Southeast Asia country that joined the *Treaty of Amity and Cooperation in Southeast Asia* (TAC). Since the implementation of *Trade in Goods Agreement of a Framework Agreement for Overall Economic Cooperation* between China and SEAN in 2005, more than 7,000 kinds of goods in bilateral trade began to enjoy tariff reduction, booming bilateral trade by large scale. In 2010, China-ASEAN Free

Trade Zone was built up and it is the largest free trade area of the developing countries across the world. After ASEAN became the biggest trade partner for ASEAN in 2009, the trade volume between the two sides has increased continuously, surpassing US$ 400 billion in 2012. China has proposed to create an upgraded version of the China-ASEAN Free Trade Area in the economic area and make a "diamond decade" in the future.

President Xi Jinping attended the 21st informal summit of the Asia-Pacific Economic Cooperation (APEC) forum in Indonesia and paid state official visits to Indonesia and Malaysia in October 2013. While in Indonesia, Xi put forward the idea of building the Maritime Silk Road of the 21st century. He said China is ready to expand its practical cooperation with ASEAN countries across the board, supplying each other's needs and complementing each other's strengths, with a view to jointly seizing opportunities and meeting challenges for the benefit of common development and prosperity. In the same month Premier Li

In October 2013, the 16th ASEAN + 3 (China, Japan and South Korea) Summit was held in Bandar Seri Begawan, capital of Brunei and Premier Li Keqiang attended the summit.

In September 2013, the 13th meeting of the Council of the Heads of the Member States of the Shanghai Cooperation Organization was held in Kyrgyzstan. President Xi Jinping attended the meeting.

Keqiang proposed at the 16th ASEAN-China (10+1) Summit that China is ready to discuss with ASEAN the signing of the treaty of good-neighborliness and friendly cooperation between China and ASEAN countries so as to consolidate the political foundation for China-ASEAN strategic mutual trust.

Second are its relations with Northwest countries. In order to explore means to settle their boundary issues left over from history, the heads of state from China, Russia, Kazakhstan, Kyrgyzstan and Tajikistan met in Shanghai and Moscow in 1996 and 1997, reaching agreements to strengthen confidence-building in the military fields and disarmament in the border regions. These meetings launched the annual meeting mechanism of the Shanghai Five, which not only facilitated the peaceful settlement of the boundary issues between them left over from history but also increased mutual trust among member states, and extended the mutual beneficial cooperation among them from security area to political, diplomatic, economic, and cultural fields.

The fruitful cooperation among the Shanghai Five led to the establishment of the Shanghai Cooperative Organization (SCO) in 2001. Since its inception, the SCO internally has pursued the Shanghai spirit of mutual trust, mutual benefits, and equality, as well as respecting the diversity of civilization and seeking mutual development. China has been persistent on the principles of non-alignment, inclusiveness, not targeting other countries or regions. While it has enhanced cooperation among member states, the influence of the SCO has also been on the rise. In addition to China, Russia, Kazakhstan, Kyrgyzstan, Tajikistan and Uzbekistan, the SCO has admitted Mongolia, Pakistan, Iran, Afghanistan, and India as observers, Sri Lanka, Belo Russia and Turkey as dialogue partners, Turkmenistan and Commonwealth of Independent States (CIS) as guest participants. SCO has become an important platform to maintain regional security in China's northwest and for the member states to increase trust. It also helped to propel the economic and trade relation between China and the Central Asia countries. The total trade volume between China and Central Asia climbed in 2012 to $46 billion - 100 times the volume in 1992, the year China forged diplomatic relations with the region's five nations.

In September 2013, President Xi participated in the 13th summit of the SCO in Bishkek, Kyrgyzstan and paid official state visits to Turkmenistan, Kazakhstan, Uzbekistan and Kyrgyzstan. While in Kazakhstan Xi made the official suggestion for building the Silk Road Economic Belt Zone through accelerating policy communication, improving road connectivity, promoting unimpeded trade, enhancing monetary circulation and enhancing understanding. The plan is intended to promote economic links further cemented and cooperation further deepened among Asian and European countries by fanning out the cooperation from point to area and from strip to large scope.

Third are its relations with Southwest countries. The frequent visits between Chinese leaders and Indian and Pakistani leaders have led to the improved Sino-Indian relations and the consolidated traditional friendship between China and Pakistan.

China and India engaged in war over territorial difference and the two sides have not found a solution for the 130,000 square km disputed territory. However, the bilateral relations gradually improved after the end of the Cold War and they have signed three bilateral agreements, including the *Agreement on the Maintenance of Peace and Tranquility along the Line of Actual Control in the India-China Border Areas* (1993), the *Agreement on Confidence Building Measures in the Military Field along the Line of Actual Control in the India-China Border Areas* (1996), and the *Agreement on the Political Parameters and Guiding Principles for the Settlement of the Boundary Question* (2005). The leaders of China and India confirmed in 2000 to forge a strategic partnership oriented to the 21st century, and the two sides further signed the *Joint Declaration on Principles for Relations and Comprehensive Co-operation* in 2003, agreeing to maintain the status quo pending the final resolution of Sino-Indian boundary

On November 28, 2013, Urumchi Silk Road Economic Belt Cities Cooperation and Development Forum was held with 300 guests from 24 cities of seven countries along the Silk Road to conduct exchanges and dialogues on the relevant topics.

issue. At the same time, the two sides agreed to designate their respective representatives to explore the framework for the final settlement of the boundary issues. And it has had 16 rounds of talks as of June 2013. During Indian Prime Minister Prime Minister Manmohan Singh's visit to China, the two sides signed a *Border Defense Cooperation Agreement* in which the two sides committed to maintain peace, stability and tranquility along the Line of actual control.

As Sino-India political relations improved their cooperation expanded to security domain. From 2003 to 2008, the two sides had five joint military exercises. Bilateral trade began to climb reaching US$ 61.74 billion in 2010 and US$ 73.9 billion in 2011. Due to the drop in India's export to China their bilateral trade dropped to US$ 66.47 billion in 2012. The great potential in bilateral economic relations remains unexplored. In addition to bilateral cooperation the two sides maintain close consultation and coordination in the informal summit of BRIICS and G20, within the WTO and the UN, and the Conferences on Climate Change.

In October 2003, Premier Li Keqiang and Prime Minister Manmohan Singh of Indonesia attended the bilateral document signing ceremony in Beijing.

Meanwhile, China established all-weather friendship relations with Pakistan and the two sides have been engaging in cooperation in all directions. Politically, the two parties maintain close cooperation and the leaders of the two countries exchanged visit frequently. The two countries announce to build closer strategic cooperative partnership during Premier Wen Jiabao's visit to Pakistan in 2005. During Premier Li Keqiang's visit to Pakistan in May 2013, the two countries issued a Joint Statement, which affirmed the accomplishments in their bilateral relations and drew up the blueprint their future development.

Sound bilateral political relations paved the way for cooperation in other fields. One of them is close cooperation in security area. China and Pakistan jointly developed a production line in 2007 which have produced 50 JF-17 Thunder fighter planes in 2013 and the two sides have agreed to produce 50 more. Bilateral trade also increased gradually after China and Pakistan signed a free trade agreement in 2006 and the bilateral trade reached $12.4 billion in 2012, up 17.6 percent from 2011. The two countries supported each other on international affairs. Pakistan extended full support to China on Taiwan, Tibet, human rights issues and opposed Western countries' interference in China's internal affairs. China supported Pakistan in safeguarding its national security and opposing external interference. The two countries also maintained cooperation and supported each other on counter terrorism and have held joint exercises on counter-terrorism.

China's diplomatic efforts to its Southwest only promoted China's relations with India and Pakistan, the two important developing countries and greatly contributed to regional peace greatly improved the security environment in its Southwest area.

Last are its relations with Northeast countries. After the Korean nuclear issue escalated into a crisis, China engaged in a shuttle diplomacy and good offices by dispatching its envoys to countries concerned, persuading the six parties—the DPRC, the U.S., the ROC, Japan, Russia, and China—to come to

China and Pakistan joined hand to develop Xiaolong Fighter.

the negotiation table. During this process, China hosted each round of talks, provided facilities, chaired each session, and motivated the parties to set the final goal of denuclearizing the Korean Peninsula. China insisted that the North Korean nuclear issues should be settled through dialogue and peaceful means to avoid the Korean nuclear issue from running out of control. China's diplomatic efforts not only contributed to regional peace but were conducive to the security environment in Northeast Asia.

China's surrounding areas are full of dynamics with remarkable advantage and potential in development. With power shift in this area, traditional and non-traditional security issues, old problems concerning perception on history and newly emerged maritime disputes have brought about crisis of different kind in this area. Among them are Diaoyu Islands issue and the maritime disputes over the South China Sea, which concern China's territory sovereignty. The Chinese government put China's national interest as the first priority and has acted firmly to uphold its sovereignty, security and territorial integrity while it stood ready to appropriately handle and resolve these disputes with relevant neighboring countries through direct bilateral dialogue and negotiation. This is also the experience how China settled its land boundary disputes with the majority of its neighbors.

The Status Quo of Boundary Issues Between China and Its Neighbors		
Border disputes that have been settled and major agreement of the settlement	China-Myanmar	Sino-Burmese Agreement on Boundary Issue (1960) Sino-Burmese Boundary Treaty (1960)
	China-Nepal	Sino-Nepalese Agreement on Question of Boundary between the Two Countries (1960) Sino-Nepalese Boundary Treaty (1961)
	China-Korea	Sino-Korean Boundary Treaty (1962) Sino-Korean Boundary Protocol (1964)
	China-Mongolia	Sino-Mongolian Border Treaty (1962)
	China-Pakistan	Sino-Pak Agreement on the Boundary Between China's Xinjiang and the Contiguous Areas the Defense of Which Is Under the actual Control of Pakistan (1963)
	China-Afghanistan	Sino-Afghan Boundary Treaty (1963)
	China-Russia	Sino-Soviet Agreement on the Eastern Section of the Boundary Between China and Soviet Union (1991) Sino-Russian Agreement on the Western Section of the Boundary Between China and Russia (1994) Protocol on the Eastern Section and the Western Section of the Boundary Between China and Russia (1999) Supplementary Boundary Agreement on the Eastern Section of the Boundary Between China and Russia (2004) Sino-Russia Supplementary Boundary Agreement on the Eastern Section of the Boundary Between China and Russia and Attached Maps (2008)

	China-Laos	Sino-Lao Boundary Treaty (1991)
Border disputes that have been settled and major agreement of the settlement	China-Vietnam	The Sino-Vietnamese Land Boundary Treaty (1999) The Sino-Vietnamese Agreement on Maritime Boundary Delimitation in the Gulf of Tonkin, Special Economic Zone and Continental Shelf (2000)
	China-Kazakhstan	Boundary Agreement Between China and Kazakhstan (1994) The Supplementary Boundary Agreement Between China and Kazakhstan (1997)
	China-Kyrgyzstan	Sino-Kyrgyz Agreement on Sino-Kyrgystan Boundary Issue (1996) The Supplementary Boundary Agreement Between China and Kyrgyzstan (1998)
	China-Tajikistan	Sino-Tajik Boundary Treaty (1999) The Supplementary Boundary Agreement Between China and Tajikistan (2002)
Disputes with provincial Agreements	China-India	Sino-Indian Agreement on the Maintenance of Peace and Tranquility along the Line of Actual Control in the India-China Border Areas (1993) Sino-Indian Agreement on Confidence Building Measures in the Military Field along the Line of Actual Control in the India-China Border Areas (1996)
	China-Bhutan	Sino-Bhutan Agreement on Maintenance of Peace and Tranquility in China-Bhutan Border Area (1998)
Disputes without any formal agreement	China-Japan	Diaoyu Islands
	China-Philippine, Vietnam Brunei, Malaysia	the islands in the South China Sea and its adjacent waters and maritime right

The root of the current disputes between China and Japan over the Diaoyu Islands lies in the Japanese government's action to "nationalize" Diaoyu Islands, which went against the bilateral consensus on "shelve the disputes" and changed the status quo in fact. The Chinese side insists that Japan must correct its mistake and return to the consensus the two sides reached earlier and recognize the fact that disputes exist between China and Japan over the Diaoyu Islands. When this condition is met, China is willing to seek means of crisis management or settlement of the disputes through dialogues and negotiation.

China has legal, historical and factual evidence to enjoy indisputable sovereignty over Nansha (Spratly) Islands and Xisha (Paracel) Islands and its adjacent waters. In response to some countries recent territorial claim over some of these islands which stirred up the disputes, the Chinese government enhanced its presence in this area and established the Sansha City. As for the international side of the issue, China stands ready to seek proper settlement of the issue with relevant countries through equal-footed dialogue and friendly consultation in the overall interests of bilateral ties and regional stability on the basis of fully respecting the reality and international law. Pending their final settlement shelve the disputes. However, China is opposed to taking the issue to international arbitration or introduces external forces to this issue or the intervention of external forces.

Enhancing Solidarity and Cooperation with Other Developing Countries

Developing countries mainly concentrate in Asia, Africa, and Latin America, and most of them share with China similar historical sufferings, identical situations and common desires, which provide a solid basis for good bilateral relations between China and other developing countries. China puts a great emphasis on its relations with other developing countries. The history of New China's relations with the majority of developing countries is one of mutual

From December 1963 to February 1964, Premier Zhou Enlai and Chen Yi, Deputy Premier and Foreign Minister, visited 13 countries of Asia and Africa. That was an important milestone for China to develop the friendship with Asian and African countries. The picture is of the group photo of Zhou Enlai, Chen Yi and Ahmed Sékou Touré, president of Guinea.

support, mutual assistance and solidarity and coordination.

Upon the funding of the New China, it has offered support of internationalism to those national liberation struggles that were going on in developing countries. From late 1960, China's assistance to the majority of developing countries in Asia and Africa was big in scale, large in amount, diverse in form and has great influence. The newly independent nationalist countries offered timely support to China in return.

China has made it the cornerstone and starting point of its foreign relations to strengthen solidarity and cooperation with other developing countries since its reform and opening-up, and has endeavored to explore new ways and means to promote mutually beneficial bilateral cooperation with other developing countries. China has supported and actively participated in South-South cooperation. The cooperation between China and other developing countries has been substantiated in content and expanded in scale, forming a situation of win-win cooperation.

Since the beginning of this century, China has consistently considered it one pillar of its overall foreign relations to develop relations with the majority of developing countries. The Political Report to the 18th CPC National Congress in 2013 points out, China "will increase unity and cooperation with other developing countries, work with them to uphold the legitimate rights and interests of developing countries and support efforts to increase their representation and voice in international affairs. China will remain a reliable friend and sincere partner of other developing countries." In the first thirteen years of the 21 century, China has provided assistance to more than 120 developing countries within the framework of South-South Cooperation and has built 200 plus schools, more than 30 hospitals and counter-malaria centers, and has trained 80,000 professionals.

Soon after he assumed Presidency in 2013 Xi Jinping has visited Africa and Latin America. He has held bilateral and multilateral meetings with leaders of dozens of countries and has signed a series of big projects concerning national economy and people's livelihood in Africa, upgrading the new type of Sino-African strategic partnership to a new level. He revealed a series of new measures to support Caribbean countries' economic and social development, further promoted China's cooperation with Latin America to new heights. In order to promote solidarity and cooperation among new emerging economies and developing countries, China give impetus to establish a development bank and a contingent reserve arrangement among BRICS countries, thus adding momentum and dynamics to the new cooperative platform for developing countries. Due to the differences in their respective condition, China's relations with developing countries in different continents had different experiences and demonstrate remarkable features.

China's relations with African and Arab countries

The relations between China and African and Arab countries started from the first Asian-African Conference held in Bandung, Indonesia in 1955. Chinese Premier Zhou Enlai put forward at this conference the principle of seeking common ground while putting aside differences, which dismissed the concerns and misunderstandings of some developing countries about China. China established diplomatic ties with Egypt in 1956, a significant start in its relations with African and Arab countries. To date, China has established diplomatic ties with all Arab countries and 48 of the 53 African countries.

China and the majority of the African and Arab countries have rendered mutual support in history. China has firmly supported their desire in upholding national independence and pursuing national economic development. During his visit to 10 Asian and African countries from December 1963 to February 1964, Premier Zhou Enlai put forward five principles guiding China's relations with African and Arab countries and eight principles for China's aid to African countries. The Tanzara Railway constructed with a RMB 988 million an interest-free loan from the Chinese government is a historical monument of friendship between China and Africa.

Tanzania-Zambia Railway - a well-known foreign-aid project of China. Started construction in 1970, the railway was completed in 1976. It is 1860km long and a traffic trunk connecting East Africa and the middle and south Africa.

African countries have always supported China to restore its lawful seat in the UN. 26 of the 76 countries that voted in the 26th session of the UN General Assembly in 1971 for the resolution to restore China's legitimate rights in the UN were from Africa. The late Chairman Mao Zedong humored that "it is our African friends who have brought us back to the United Nations."

Once China had its legitimate rights in the UN restored, China has stood firmly by the side of the developing countries. For instance, China voted 16 times in succession for the candidate Salim Ahmed Salim, Tanzanian Foreign Minister, to be elected during the election for UN Secretary-General in 1982. Although Salim failed to be elected as anticipated, the new Secretary-General, Javier Perez de Cuellar, was also from a developing country. In 1991, China worked energetically to support African countries in the election of the UN Secretary-General leading to the election of Boutros-Ghali, Egyptian vice Prime Minister, as the Secretary-General of the United Nations.

After the policy of reform and opening-up, the new Chinese Premier made his first trip to Africa, where he put forward four principles on expanding economic and trade relations with developing countries, namely, equality and mutual benefit, stress on practical results, diversity in form, and attainment of common progress. Sino-African relations witnessed a transformation from struggling for independence to seek development, greatly expanded the channels of the bilateral relations.

Further progress has been made in Sino-African relations since the end of the Cold War. Nine heads of state from Sub-Saharan African countries visited China in 1989 alone. During his visit to six African countries in 1996, Chinese President Jiang Zemin put forward a five-point proposal for the development of a 21st century-oriented long-term stable China-Africa relationship of all-around cooperation: to treat each other as equals, develop sincere friendship, strengthen solidarity and cooperation, and seek common development.

In March 2013, President Xi Jinping made a state visit to Tanzania and was warmly welcomed by the local people.

Upon assuming Presidency Xi included Africa in his first foreign trip. In his speech at Tanzania, President Xi used "sincerity, real results, affinity and good faith" to characterize China's Africa policy in the new era. China supports African countries to explore developing paths that fit their own national situation and he expressed his confidence in the future of Africa.

To jointly meet the challenges in the new century, China, motivated by some African countries, proposed the establishment of the Forum on China–Africa Cooperation, which has become a new mechanism Sino-African collective dialogue within the framework of South-South Cooperation and a new platform to strengthen Sino-Africa consultation and cooperation. It held ministerial meeting every three years to lay out the blueprint and promote Sino-Africa cooperation to a new stage. For instance, one of the eight pledges China made at the FOCAC Beijing Summit is the establishment of the China-Africa Development Fund, which had invested US$ 2.385 billion in 61 projects in 30 African countries, and had invested US$ 1.806 billion for 53 projects by the end of 2012.

Forum on China–Africa Cooperation

The first ministerial meeting was held in Beijing in October 2000, which passed the *Beijing Declaration of the Forum on China–Africa Cooperation* and the *Programme for China–Africa Cooperation in Economic and Social Development*. China pledged to package measures of assistance to Africa.

The second ministerial meeting was held in Addis Ababa Ethiopia December 2003, which passed the *FOCAC Addis Ababa Action Plan (2004–2006)*. China pledged to increase its foreign aid to Africa in the next three years from 2004 to 2006.

The FOCAC Summit and the third ministerial conference were held in Beijing in November, 2006, which passed *FOCAC Beijing*

Declaration and *FOCAC Bejing Action Plan* (2007–2009) ,and China rolled out 8 measures of assistance to Africa.

The fourth ministerial meeting was held in Sharm El-Sheikh, Egypt in Nov. 2009, which passed the *Sharm el-Sheikh Declaration* and *FOCAC Sharm El-Sheikh Action Plan for 2010–2012* to chart the path for further China–Africa cooperation.

The fifth Ministerial Meeting was held in Beijing July 2012 which passed the *Beijing Declaration* and *FOCAC Fifth Ministerial Meeting Beijing Action Plan.*

Sino-African mutual beneficial economic relations have been further expanded in the 21st century. After China became Africa's No. 1 trade partner in 2009, the scale of China-Africa trade expanded rapidly. In 2012, the total volume of China-Africa trade reached US$ 198.49 billion. Africa is now China's major import source, second largest overseas construction project contract market and fourth largest investment destination. As of 2013, over 2,000 Chinese enterprises are investing and developing in more than 50 African countries and regions. From 2009 to 2012, China's direct investment in Africa increased from US$ 1.44 billion to US$ 2.52 billion, with an annual growth rate of 20.5%. Over the same period, China's accumulative direct investment in Africa increased from US$9.33 billion to US$ 21.23 billion. Sino-African economic and trade cooperation has helped the improvement of African people's live and facilitated diversification of African economy. At the same time, it has provided a forceful support to China's economic and social development and contributed to the balanced development of the world economy. It sets a model of South-South Cooperation.

People to people and cultural exchanges make up an important part of the new type of strategic partnership between China and Africa and are an important pillar of bilateral relations. By supporting young Africans studying in China, sending young Chinese volunteers to Africa and developing joint research initiatives, China tries to promote mutual understanding between China and African countries and strengthen the social foundation of their friendship. From 2010 to 2012, China granted 18,743 government scholarships to students from African countries. From 2010 to 2012, China held various training courses for 54 countries and regions in Africa; the courses involved a total of 27,318 officials and technicians. Twenty pairs of leading Chinese and African universities have begun cooperating under the 20+20 Cooperation Plan for Chinese and African Universities. From the launch of China-Africa Joint Research and Exchange Plan in March 2010 to the end of 2012, it had supported 64 projects in the form of workshops, subject research, academic exchanges, and publishing works. The project had also subsidized visits and exchanges for over 600 Chinese and African scholars.

The Sino-Arabic Forum was founded in 2004 following the success with the Forum on China-Africa Cooperation. The forum has become a new mechanism to strengthen Sino-Arabic dialogue and cooperation. Under this mechanism, China and Arab countries have taken vigorous measures on promoting bilateral

In July 2012, the Fifth Ministerial Conference of FOCAC was held in Beijing.

exchanges and cooperation in such fields as economy and trade, investment, energy, education, culture, science and technology, public health and environment, so as to attain common development of the two sides.

China's relations with Latin American countries

China and Latin American countries are all developing countries. Due to the long distance between them and the differences in their respective geographical conditions, social systems, and cultural traditions, New China's relations with Latin American countries started relatively late. However, the relations have developed very fast once started, and have soon become an important part of China's external relations.

Latin America has traditionally been referred to as the "backyard" of the U.S. Except for Sino-Cuban diplomatic relations which was normalized in 1960, no breakthrough in China's relations with the rest of the Latin American countries was made until the rapprochement in Sino-US in the early 1970s when 11 Latin American countries established diplomatic relations with China consecutively.

Strengthening solidarity and cooperation with other developing countries, including Latin American countries, has been the cornerstone of China's foreign relations since its reform and opening-up. The head of the Chinese government paid a first visit to Latin America in 1985 when he introduced four guidelines for China's relations with Latin American, namely, peace and friendship, mutual support, equality and mutual benefit and attainment of common progress. During this visit, as many as 15 agreements, cooperating on politics, economy, trade, science and technology, culture, and financial issues, were concluded between China and Columbia, Brazil, Argentina and Venezuela, laying a solid foundation for China's friendly relations with Latin American countries in various fields. Since then, Sino-Latin American relations have revealed a new situation of comprehensive development, both governmental and people-to-people cooperation.

Acceleration with the process of globalization since the end of the Cold War has shortened the distance between China and Latin American countries, and Sino-Latin American relations were further strengthened. Chinese President Jiang Zemin paid a visit to Mexico in 1997, and six countries—Chile, Argentina, Uruguay, Cuba, Venezuela and Brazil—in 2001. From 1996 to 2004, eight presidents, three governors and three premiers from Latin American developing countries paid friendly visits to China. Exchanges of visits between top leaders from the two sides greatly have consolidated the bilateral cooperation between China and Latin American countries.

The 21st century witnesses the new progress of the relations between China and the Latin American countries, featuring continuous exchanges of high-level visits, strengthened political ties, and new progress in economic and trade cooperation. President Hu Jintao paid visits to Brazil, Argentina, Chile and Cuba in 2004 and Costa Rica, Cuba and Peru in 2008. Chinese Foreign Ministry issued *China's Policy Paper on Latin America and the Caribbean* in 2008, which elaborated the goal and fields of cooperation in China's relations with Latin America, put forward the guiding principle for Sino-Latin American cooperation, and laid a more solid foundation for the comprehensive development of Sino-Latin American relations.

In the first year after assuming the presidency, Xi Jinping paid state official visits to Trinidad and Tobago, Costa Rica and Mexico and held talks with leaders of eight Caribbean countries that have diplomatic ties with China. During the same year, nine heads of state or heads of government from Mexico, Peru, Venezuela, Uruguay, Jamaica, Antigua and Barbuda, Surinam, Dominic, Bolivia visited China. The important consensus reached between Chinese and Latin American leaders during these visit to further cement their bilateral relations in the new era laid solid political foundation and added new momentum for the development of the bilateral relations.

At present, China has maintained diplomatic ties with 21 of the 33 Latin American countries. Since its establishment of a "strategic partnership" with Brazil in 1993, China has set up a "strategic partnership for future common development" with Venezuela, a "strategic partnership" with Mexico, Argentina and Peru, and a "strategic partnership of common development" with Chile. The political consultation between China and Latin American countries has been further institutionalized and the dialogue mechanisms are being improved. Sino-Latin American Forum for Think-Tank Exchanges, Sino-Latin American Forum for Legal Cooperation, China and Latin American Caribbean People's Friendship Association and other non-official mechanisms are playing effective roles in strengthening bilateral relations.

China has also worked together with Latin America in a multilateral arena. China became an observer in Inter-America Development Bank and in Latin American Integration Association in 1991 and 1993 respectively. Thereafter,

In June 2013, President Xi Jinping attended the commencement ceremony of Trinidad and Tobago Children's Hospital undertaken by the Chinese developers, accompanied by Trinidad and Tobago Primer Minister Bisaisaer, during his state visit to the country.

China became an observer in the Organization of American States and the United Nations Economic Commission for Latin America successively in 2000 and 2004. In addition, China has also launched dialogue mechanisms with the Rio Group, Southern African Development Community (SADC) and the Andean Group, and established foreign ministerial consultation mechanisms with major Latin American countries, forming multi-channel and effective communication mechanisms. China and major Latin American countries maintain close communication and coordination during the informal summits of BRICS, G20, APECT and other mechanisms.

Strong political relations create favorable conditions for economic and trade cooperation between China and major Latin American countries. China has signed agreements on economic and technology cooperation or economic cooperation with 16 Latin American countries, agreements on investment encouragement and mutual investment protection with 11 countries, treaties on avoiding double taxation with five Latin American countries. China and Chile, Peru, Costa Rica have reached free trade agreements, which are now smoothly implemented. The feasibility of free trade agreement with Columbia has been initiated. All of these instruments have facilitated the remarkable achievements on Sino-Latin American economic and trade cooperation. For instance, the trade volume between China and Latin American countries was only $1 billion in 1979. That volume reached US$ 261.2 billion, accounting for 6.8% of China's total foreign trade in the year of 2012, making China the second largest trade partner of Latin America. At the same time Latin America is the area whose trade with China grows the fastest.

In cultural domain, China has established 32 Confucius Institutes and 10 Confucius Classroom in 14 Latin America and Caribbean countries and the Chinese Culture Center has been established in Mexico. China has offered 5000 scholarships for Latin American and Caribbean countries in the five years from 2012 and more and more Chinese students are going to Latin America for further

In April 2014, Wang Yi, Minister of Foreign Affairs of China, held talks with the visiting delegation of the Community of Latin American and Caribbean States in Beijing.

study. The 21 countries in Latin America and Caribe area that have diplomatic relations with China have all become the tourism destination countries.

Sino-Latin American economic and trade cooperation continues to develop in various fields with an increasingly solid foundation. It has come to the best time in history in terms of speed of growth, width and depth of cooperation. The role of Latin American countries in China's foreign relations is on the rise and will become more and more important in the future.

Adapting to Globalization, and Promoting Comprehensive Diplomacy

The globalization of the world today is a comprehensive and multi-level process. In the economic sphere, almost all countries have chosen a market economy as their mode of economic development regardless of their different social systems and development status. International trade and global investment have expanded at an unprecedented speed in both geographical distribution and scale, making the world an intertwined global market.

In the process of economic globalization, new means of communication based on high technology has not only shortened the distance between countries and regions, but also provided the material foundation for the globalization of production and market, and brought about information globalization. Meanwhile, the extensive employment of modern transportation tools has made long-distance travel possible within a short time, and cross-border migration of people has been on the rise day by day. The world we live in has become a global village.

On September 27, 2013, Wang Yi, Minister of Foreign Affairs of China, made a speech at the General Debate of the UN General Assembly to introduce the diplomatic philosophy and ideas of the new administration of China.

Globalization has made countries intimately connected and interdependent. It has not only changed the relationship between internal and external affairs, and blurred their boundaries, but also changed the environment, issues, methods and means, and even the content and concept of diplomacy. Diplomatic agendas are becoming increasingly pluralized, expanding from the conventional political and military realms to that of economy and culture. The subjects of diplomacy have expanded from sovereign state actors to encompass international organizations, transnational corporations, as well as political parties, parliaments, and non-governmental organizations. Changes are also taking place with diplomatic means and channels.

China regards globalization neither as "a panacea for all development problems" or "a scourge inevitably leading to disaster." Instead, it is considered "an objective trend of world economic development independent of man's will, and no country can bypass it." "No nation would be able to develop its economy by isolation from the rest of the world." In the light of its national conditions and the calling of the times, China has put forward the scientific outlook featuring people-oriented, all-around, coordinated and sustainable development. In foreign affairs, China has unswervingly adhered to the opening-up policy and actively participated in international economic cooperation and competition in conformity with the development of globalization. It has brought forth the concept of "grand diplomacy," or "comprehensive diplomacy" in foreign affairs and conducted multi-areas, multi-level and multi-channel foreign relations.

Broadened Diplomatic Arena

Promoting economic diplomacy

The third plenary session of the 11th Central Committee of the CPC in 1978 decided to shift the focus from domestic work to economic construction. Thereafter, the relationship between internal and external affairs changed from a policy of domestic politics serving foreign policy goals, to one that said foreign policy is to serve domestic policy. The policies also sought to create a sound international and neighboring environment for domestic economic development. With regard to the relationship between politics and economics, "politics in command" gave way to the idea that politics should serve the economy, rather

In December 2001, China officially joined the World Trade Organization, indicating that China has become an important part of the world economic system.

than the opposite, or with equal importance given to politics and economy. The significance of China's economic diplomacy began to be revealed.

As reform and opening-up gathered momentum, China made efforts to promote foreign trade, expand international cooperation, amend domestic laws to encourage foreign investment and introduce advanced technology. China's seats in the World Bank and International Monetary Fund (IMF) was restored, it joined the Asian Development Bank, and began to apply for the restoration of its seat in General Agreement on Tariffs and Trade (GATT). All these economic activities enlarged China's openness and strengthened its closer ties with the world, which inserted a strong impetus to the country's economic growth and enhanced its strength. China's economic diplomacy has scored a remarkable achievement.

Economic globalization has continued surging ahead since the end of the Cold War, presenting China with unprecedented challenges and opportunities in its cause of reform and opening-up as well as its modernization drive. It was to the clear realization of the Chinese government that prosperity could be sought only if it followed the major tide through vigorous participation in the international community. China stepped up the process to integrate into the international economic system, joined the APEC and applied to enter the WTO and other international multilateral economic organizations. The idea of economic diplomacy has become more explicit.

The significance of economic diplomacy was further upgraded in China's overall foreign relations since the 21st century and has drawn much attention from the decision-makers. Economic diplomacy has been brought into the overall strategy of national economic and social development, embodied in China's omni-directional foreign relations structure. It has become an effective way to promote China's national interests and an important platform to enhance China's relations with different countries. In view of the changing situation, the Chinese Foreign Ministry, following the establishment of the International Economic

Department in 2012, formed a Consultative Committee for Economic and Financial Affairs in December 2013 to reinforce economic diplomacy.

First of all, promoting economic diplomacy has been done by cementing China's economic ties, developing cooperation and avoiding confrontation, and by stabilizing bilateral relations with West countries so as to ensure the necessary market for China's economic development. EU, the U.S. and Japan and other developed counties are China's major trade partners. Mutually beneficial cooperation on an equal footing in the economic field and rising bilateral trade volumes have become the cornerstones of China's relations with EU, the United States, and Japan.

Secondly, economic diplomacy has become the important means by which China has strengthened its relations with other developing countries. The Chinese government held a national conference on China's economic diplomacy toward developing countries in 2004. The conference emphasized that we should "combine friendly and mutual trust relations in the political field with cooperation

In September 2013, the 3rd China-Eurasia Expo was held in Urumchi, Xinjiang.

and exchanges in the economic field to promote economic ties through political means, and coordinate economic and political relations." It also emphasized that "economic cooperation should be carried out in a diversified manner with a focus on practical effect, and combine trade with investment, foreign aid funds with credit funds, as well as the strategy of 'going out' with 'inviting in'." Since the beginning of the new century, China's trade with ASEAN, new emerging economies, and other developing countries have witnessed a steady and fast growth. With adjusted policies and new means to enhance bilateral relations, the basis of China's relations with other developing countries has shifted from cooperation in anti-imperialism, anti-colonialism, striving for and safeguarding national independence, to mutually beneficial economic cooperation.

Thirdly, another major aspect of China's economic diplomacy has been China's integration with the global economic mechanisms and participation in global economic cooperation. China has made efforts for 15 years since its application for the restoration of its GATT contracting status in 1986 to its final accession to WTO in October 2001. During the process, China speeded up domestic reforms on the one hand and insisted on the principle of balancing rights and obligations in its negotiation with the WTO China group on the other hand. China integrates into the world further which creates a favorable external environment for the continued rapid growth of China's economy.

To honor its commitments upon entry into the WTO, China expanded its opening-up in the fields of industry, agriculture and the services trade, and accelerated trade and investment facilitation and liberalization. China expedited improvements to the legal system for foreign economic relations and trade and reviewed over 2,300 laws and regulations, and departmental rules and abolished or revised those that did not accord with WTO rules and China's commitments upon entry into the WTO. China has taken further measures to lower tariffs and reduce non-tariff measures. During the transitional period following China's entry into the WTO, the general level of China's import tariffs was lowered

from 15.3 percent in 2001 to 9.9 percent in 2005. Other measures include fully liberalizing access to foreign trade operations. Further opening the services market creating a level playing field.

Fourth, China has been vigorously engaging in multilateral economic dialogues and developing free-trade zones with other countries. Chinese leaders have exchanged views with leaders of other countries and personages from the business circle to reach a better understanding and have ended up with important projects of cooperation. By the end of 2012 China has established and maintained business and trade ties with 163 countries and regions. It has signed ten free-trade-zone agreements, bilateral investment treaties with 129 countries, and double taxation avoidance agreements with 96 countries. All this shows that China is actively promoting liberalization and facilitation of trade and investment. Furthermore, since its first participation in the G8 dialogue meeting with the major developing countries in 2003, China has kept in close touch with the G8. China has elaborated its views during the dialogue on such important issues as the energy and the environment, and played a constructive role in solving global economic problems.

Fifth, in conformity with the ever-changing situation of the world economy, international cooperation in such fields as energy, climate change and environment has become the new areas in China's economic diplomacy. The Chinese government has paid great importance to the challenges of global climate change facing mankind. The Chinese government has set up a national leading works group in tackling the problem of climate change, energy saving and pollution reduction, and has formulated the *National Program on Tackling Climate Change*. On the international platform, China has been working harder to promote international cooperation on climate change and has called on developed countries to extend financial and technological support to developing countries in their effort to address climate change.

On the energy issue, China has proposed that cooperation should take the

The equipment such as high-speed railway with higher content of technology is expected to become the new strong powerhouse of economic growth of China.

place of competition, and advocated full cooperation among countries in the spirit of mutual benefit to create a win-win or all-win scenario. The "Eleventh Five-Year Plan (2006−2010)" of China's economic and social development approved in 2006 stated explicitly that China would increase its overseas cooperation in halting oil and gas exploitation on the basis of equality and mutual benefit, reaching a win-win result. China should ensure a safe supply of energy by actively engaging in the international energy system and making full use of the international market. Building on the experiences of other countries, China has followed a mode that prioritized friendly political relations, with emphasis on economic and trade relations. China has also supplied economic aid and other means to guarantee a stable and viable energy supply for China's domestic economic progress by establishing comprehensive cooperative partnership with energy-producing countries.

High-speed railway diplomacy

The main task of China's economic diplomacy is to expand economic cooperation, promote common development, push on China's export and create a sound external environment for domestic economic construction. High speed rail line diplomacy demonstrates the new features of China's economic diplomacy and its role in China's overall diplomacy.

China is country with a big population and railway transportation occupies an important role in national construction. After consecutive raises in train speed China decided to develop its high-speed railway from the beginning of this century and the length has surpassed 10,000 kilometer in the last ten years (till 2013), the longest in the world. China has accumulated rich experience constructing and operating high-speed railways and its technology also matured. During President Xi and Premier Li' s visit to Southeast Asia in October 2013, they both championed the nation's high-speed rail technologies like "salesmen". China and Thailand signed a Memorandum of Understanding on Deepening Railway Cooperation during Premier Li's visit to Thailand. One month later, China reached an agreement with Hungary and Serbia during Premier Li's visit to East Europe for the meeting with 16 central and Eastern European countries to build a railway connecting Belgrade and Budapest. China and Romania also decided to cooperate in high-speed railway. High-speed railway diplomacy highlighted of the new administration's economic diplomacy.

High-speed railway diplomacy signals the transformation of China's export from labor intensive products to high-value added equipment and technology as China restructuring its economy.

> Cooperation in high-speed railway can upgrade the level of cooperation and improve the quality of mutual connection. It reveals the complementary and mutual-promoting relations between traditional diplomacy and economic diplomacy.

After years of development, foreign trade has become the most dynamic and fastest growing sector of China's economy. The country's total import and export volume grew from US$ 20.6 billion-worth in 1978 to US$ 3.86698 trillion-worth in 2012. Its rank in world trade has increased from number 32 in 1978 to number 2 in 2012, making China the largest trade partner of 128 countries. Utilized foreign direct investment from 1979 to 2010 totaled US$ 1.04838 trillion. At the same time China is the fasted growing exporter, most promising investment destiny, and a major importer of energy and raw materials.

Since its reform and opening-up, China has used economic diplomacy to maintain stable relations with big powers; substantiate China's relations with other developing countries; ensure the resources, markets, and capitals for China's domestic economic construction; and efficiently promote the sustained fast growth with China's economy. China's economic diplomacy will further expand in its content and means, and will play an increasingly crucial role in the country's overall diplomacy structure with the changing situation.

Carrying out cultural diplomacy

Among all ancient civilizations of the world, the Chinese civilization held an unchallenged record of continuity, which developed to date without any major interruption. External cultural exchanges have been a long tradition in Chinese history. Examples like Zhang Qian's (?–114 BC) epic journey to the Western Regions in the Han Dynasty, Xuan Zang's (602–664) travel to the India to search after the Dharma, Jian Zhen's (688–763) sailing to Japan, and Zheng He's (1371–1433) voyages to the West Seas were all of great historical significance.

"Cultural diplomacy" refers to the conducting of diplomatic civilities by sovereign states to further national cultural interests or to achieve national foreign strategy by virtue of cultural exchanges under the guidance of certain cultural policies. The emergence of this concept reflects that international cultural exchanges have moved from the conventional realm of low-politics to that of high-politics under globalization.

The purpose of diplomacy is to further national interests, first and foremost to safeguard national sovereignty, territorial integrity and national security. In this regard, the primary purpose of cultural diplomacy is also to safeguard national security. But the major and more concrete goal is put external cultural exchanges in the framework of government policy to form a favorable national image conducive to the country's overall national foreign policy.

Foreign cultural exchanges serve a key part of China's foreign relations. Constrained by the Cold War structure, China's external cultural interaction was

2010 Shanghai World Expo attracted 190 countries and 56 international organizations. The picture is the beautiful China Pavilion.

once mainly confined to socialist countries led by the Soviet Union and countries friendly to China in Asia, Africa and Latin America. The cultural exchange program for the period 1965–1966 was signed by the Chinese government and the French government in 1965 after their establishment of diplomatic ties in 1964, which was China's first intergovernmental cultural exchange program with a Western European country. It was stipulated in the Constitution, approved by the fifth session of the Fifth NPC in 1982, to conduct cultural exchanges with other countries, providing a legal assurance for ever-expanding cultural interactions. The strategy of cultural development has been included in China's national development strategies and cultural diplomacy has been recognized as important as political diplomacy and economic diplomacy for its irreplaceable position since the 21st century. The Chinese government has vigorously promoted external cultural exchanges to enhance mutual understanding between Chinese people and the peoples of the world.

Only those with national characteristics may become international. It is both the premise and basis of cultural diplomacy to secure Chinese culture in the context of globalization and consolidate the root of its traditional culture through the revival of Chinese culture and the protection of cultural heritage at the domestic level. In recent years, the Chinese government has taken measures to support public cultural projects, construct cultural infrastructure and facilities, and carry out various types of public cultural activities. Measures have also been taken in the restoration, preservation, and innovation of traditional culture, especially national folk culture.

The rejuvenation and development of Chinese culture could not be achieved without benefiting from all that is best in human civilization. In the process of opening-up, China has been open-minded to absorb all fine achievements of other cultures through drawing on others' strengths and virtues. China's opening-up policy in culture has been well indicated by the duration of foreign language fever in China, and the increasing popularity with Chinese people of Italian

opera, Broadway musicals, Russian ballet and circus, German symphony, and French painting exhibitions.

Domestic cultural preservation and revitalization pave the way for the promotion of cultural diplomacy. The ideas and theories of China's contemporary diplomacy are mainly sourced from Chinese traditional culture. China strives to uphold coexistence among various civilizations instead of conflict, dialogue instead of confrontation, interaction instead of isolation, and inclusion instead of exclusion. China also strives to learn from each other for common prosperity, all of which are deeply rooted in such thoughts of Chinese traditional culture as: "Harmony is the most precious," "The gentleman aims at harmony, but not at uniformity, while the mean man seeks uniformity rather than harmony," "Mean what you say and honor your word with real action," "Don't do unto others what you don't want others to do unto you."

Chinese Cultural Festival Programs held in Washington.

The most direct channels and means of cultural diplomacy expand external cultural exchanges with a view to China's overall diplomacy. In recent years, China's cultural diplomacy is highlighted by numerous foreign cultural interactions led by the Chinese government. By June 2009, China has set up 96 cultural offices in embassies and consulates in 82 countries, concluded intergovernmental agreements on cultural cooperation and nearly 800 annual cultural exchange implementation programs with 145 countries, and maintained close contact with hundreds of international cultural organizations. China has worked to make China understood by the rest of the world by carrying out a series of colorful cultural brand names, such as the activities of "Spring Festival," "National Day" and "Feel the Charms of Chinese Culture," which have publicized in important media internationally. Recently, China has cooperated with many countries in holding Culture Weeks, Culture Tours, Culture Festivals and Culture Years on a reciprocal terms to demonstrate the charm of profound Chinese culture on the one hand. Having promoted exchanges and mutual

Confucius Institute enables more people to learn, understand and communicate the Chinese culture.

understanding between the Chinese people and other peoples, these activities have become new ways to enhance friendships between China and relevant countries.

Language is the carrier of culture. Chinese has become one of the world's important languages with the advancement in China's status. Currently, there are more than 30 million people studying Chinese abroad in various types of educational institutions at different levels that offer Chinese language courses in approximately 100 countries. At present, more than 330 higher education institutions in China offer courses that teach Chinese as a foreign language.

An effective way to help the world understand China is by delivering Chinese culture through the establishment of the Confucius Institute. Since the opening ceremony of the first Confucius Institute overseas was held in Seoul, South Korea in 2004, 440 Confucius Institutes and 646 Confucius Classrooms have been established in 120 countries (regions) around the globe by the end of 2013. The 440 Confucius Institutes are located in 115 countries (regions), among which 93 are in 32 Asian countries (region), 37 are in 27 African countries, 149 are in 37 European countries, 114 are in 16 American countries, and 17 are in 3 Oceanic countries. 646 Confucius Classrooms are distributed in 48 countries with 50 in 13 Asian countries, 10 in African countries,153 in 18 European countries, 384 in 6 American countries, and 49 in two Oceanic countries. In addition, more than schools and institutions in different countries have applied to set up a Confucius Institute to date. More and more people in the world are getting the chance to learn and understand Chinese culture by attending Confucius Institutes and Confucius classrooms.

Confucius Institute

The flagship of China's cultural diplomacy. Its main goal is to dedicate to the demand of people of various countries around the global to study Chinese, to promote their understanding of Chinese language and culture, enhance educational exchanges between the Chinese people and the people of other countries around the world; develop friendly relations between China and other countries and promote diversification of world culture. Its main task includes teaching Chinese language, training Chinese language teacher, providing resources of Chinese language teaching, organizing Chinese language test and authenticating Chinese language teachers, providing Chinese education and cultural information consultation, and organizing language and cultural exchanges with foreign countries. (http://www.hanban.edu.cn/confuciousinstitutes/)

The Chinese government has been keen on creating conditions to facilitate non-governmental cultural exchanges and encouraging cultural enterprises to go global through proper market operations in line with international practices. Sustained and in-depth cultural diplomacy have increased mutual trust between China and its neighbors, strengthened mutual understanding between China and the western developed countries, stabilized and consolidated the traditional friendships between China and developing countries, and enhanced the relationship between China and the countries with whom China does not have diplomatic relations. Cultural diplomacy, as an important part of China's overall diplomacy, makes great contributions to and further enriches the content of it.

Conducting diplomacy for the people and protecting the lawful rights and interests of Chinese nationals and corporations overseas

Fostering the thought of "conducting diplomacy for the people" and paying attention to protecting the lawful rights and interests of Chinese nationals and corporations overseas are important parts of China's diplomacy. This implements

and puts into practice the scientific outlook on development as well as the thoughts of putting people first and governing for the people.

Protecting the lawful interests and rights of Chinese nationals abroad is an important task of the diplomatic departments accorded by the Chinese Constitution, as well as an important component of China's diplomatic works, which is professionally referred to as consular protection. The Chinese government pays great importance to developing consular relations with other countries. It stands for properly addressing the problems that may arise in bilateral consular relations through equal dialogue and friendly consultations with due consideration accorded to the concerns of each side so as to protect the legitimate rights and interests of their citizens and state, and promote consular relations affairs as well as friendships among countries. The Chinese government has followed the principles of mutual benefit and seeking win-win results through cooperation, and has maintained and developed close consultation and dialogue relations with other countries and international organizations to engage

In 2013 the number of outbound Chinese citizens reached 98.19 million, creating a record high of the outbound tourist size. The picture is of the Chinese tourist in Jeju Island of South Korea.

in extensive and in-depth discussions with open and programmatic attitudes on urgent issues of common interest in bilateral and multilateral consular relations.

The rise in cross-border mobility of people and migration is an important manifestation of globalization. With the development of globalization and China's further involvement in the international community, more and more Chinese citizens go abroad for various purposes, ranging from traveling, investing in business, studying and exporting labor services. In 2013, more than 90 million outbound visits were made by Chinese people and more than 20,000 overseas Chinese-funded institutions were set up in more than 160 countries and regions. The transformation functioned both as a bridge that helped China link with the world, and a vital symbol of China's integration into the international community. However, the complex international security situation and the growing non-traditional security threats put Chinese nationals and Chinese-funded institutions overseas under greater risks. Normalization and group-orientations are the major tendencies in cases of consular protection, which are characterized by strong political sensitivity.

The protection of the interests of Chinese nationals and corporations overseas lies in the liability of China's diplomacy. The Chinese government uses nationality as a condition of consular protection, and holds that each country should protect the lawful rights and interests of its own country and citizens as well as those of foreign nationals resided in its territory. This includes those foreign nationals who have violated the local laws, in accordance with international law, bilateral treaties and laws of the country concerned. Human treatment should be accorded when necessary and discrimination and unfair treatment should not be exercised due to their nationality, race, religion or other political or economic reasons. No countries should shield their nationals who committed offences. China is ready to cooperate with countries without diplomatic relations with China in the area of consular protection.

Following the principle of "putting prevention first and giving equal importance to prevention and the management of emergencies," the Ministry of Foreign Affairs has made use of modern technology to disseminate early warnings in consular protection. New columns of "Consular News" and "Notes on Traveling to Certain Countries and Cities" were added to the official website of the Foreign Ministry to report recent cases occurring in consular protection. Along with the issuance of *Guide of Proper Behavior for Chinese Citizens in Outbound Travel* and *Guide of Chinese Overseas Consular Protection and Service*, the website has updated travel advice, provided to deliver notes and tips of traveling to specific countries and regions, including warnings to people who are traveling to unsafe areas.

To make sure the smooth undertaking of consular protection, the Chinese government has upgraded and expanded its consular department. Early in 1955, the Department of Consular Affairs was set up under the Chinese Foreign Ministry to be in charge of consular protection operation. With the ever-increasing work of consular protection, the Consular Protection Division of the Department of Consular Affairs was upgraded to Consular Protection Center in 2007. More resources and staff were put into consular work. As a result, China has more than 240 foreign-service institutions overseas, among which 70 or so were specialized in consular affairs with the protection of the interests of overseas Chinese citizens as their main task.

Evacuating Chinese from Libya

From the beginning of this century, the foreign affairs departments of the Chinese government handle over 30,000 cases of consular protection annually, among which 17 cases are big one. The evacuation of Chinese from Libya in 2011 is the largest evacuation of overseas Chinese nationals since the founding of the New China in 1949.

From February 15, 2011, the situation in Libya gradually deteriorated and developed into a civil war in the end, threatening the lives and property of more than 30,000 Chinese working in Libya. Faced with such crisis, the State Council of China established an emergency command center on February 22 to organize and coordinate the evacuation of Chinese citizens in Libya and ensure the safety of their lives and property. The Foreign Ministry designed an emergency traveling passport and the Chinese Government sent a large number of chartered planes and rent foreign vessels, which shuttled back and forth, to withdraw Chinese nationals from Libya via the sea, land, and air. Within a short time of ten days (by 23:10 on March 2) 35,860 Chinese nationals were evacuated from Libya, 4000 per day. At the same time, China helped evacuate 2,100 people of 12 countries from strife-torn Libya.

To meet the needs of the changing situation, China's foreign affairs departments have also set up cross-sector coordination mechanisms and emergency response mechanisms. When Chinese citizens or corporations fall victim to accidents and suffer great losses overseas, an emergency response team will be constituted immediately to formulate work plans, establish hotlines, and collect information. Nowadays, China's foreign-service departments handle more than 30,000 consular protection cases of different kinds each year. Consular work has been an important part of diplomatic work and represents the thought of "conducting diplomacy for the people."

Developing military diplomacy

It is traditionally said that diplomacy starts where the war ends, indicating that military and diplomatic activities lie not in one sack. But in practice, the

military is always associated with diplomacy, and exchanges of armed forces make up one major means in enhancing mutual confidence and maintaining peace in times of peace. As an important component of its overall diplomacy, China's military diplomacy is subordinate to, and serves the national strategy of, its overall diplomacy acting as an important link promoting relations between China and other countries.

The foreign contact of the Chinese People's Liberation Army (PLA) has been a tradition of long standing. China's military diplomacy was featured with "lean to one side," the diplomatic strategy of the PRC in the wake of its founding, with its external relations confined to those with the Soviet Union and other socialist countries in Eastern Europe. During the 1960s and 1970s, the principal means of China's military diplomacy were narrowly focused on providing military assistance or training to help and support the national independence and national liberation movement of countries and peoples in the Third World.

In September 2006, the Chinese naval fleet made a friendly visit to Pearl Harbor, Hawaii. The picture is of generals of both parties at the banquet.

As China's relations with the West improved since the 1980s, the external relations of the Chinese armed forces have been enhanced, with more contacts with more countries and covering more fields. The White Paper on *China's National Defense*, issued by the Chinese government in 1998, revised the term of "foreign military contacts" to "military diplomacy" and put forward the policy of developing omni-directional and multi-level military diplomacy. The foreign relations of the PLA have experienced historic shifts from the dominance of friendly contacts at the high-level to one of pragmatic cooperation in multi-level and wide-ranging pattern, from the dominance of bilateral contacts to equal stress on both bilateral contacts and multilateral contacts, and from contacts between military professionals to omni-directional foreign contacts.

Implementing the nation's independent foreign policy of peace and its national defense policy that is purely defensive in nature, China's military diplomacy comprises military exchanges with other countries on the Five Principles of Peaceful Co-existence, with the purpose of broadening military relations and deepening military cooperation with other countries. It includes the following major aspects.

First, institutionalize the mechanism of military communications and connections. By 2008, China has established military ties with more than 150 countries, and has military attache offices in 109 countries. A total of 98 countries have military attache offices in China.

Second, develop high-level military exchanges. Exchange of military visits at the high level is the major form of military diplomacy. From 2007 to 2008, senior PLA delegations have visited more than 40 countries, and the defense ministers and chiefs of the general staff from more than 60 countries have visited China during the same period. The Chinese leaders have set great store by military diplomacy and always met with foreign military officials who were visiting China, and have actively promoted military diplomacy at summits.

Third, conduct military cooperation and exchanges in personnel development. China has sent an increasing number of military students overseas, and also accepted foreign military students to study in China. From 2007 to 2008, China sent more than 900 military students to more than 30 countries, while 20 military educational institutions in China have established and maintained inter-collegiate exchange relations with their counterparts in more than 20 countries, including the United States, Russia, Japan and Pakistan. Meanwhile, some 4,000 military personnel from more than 130 countries have come to China to study at Chinese military educational institutions.

Fourth, establish mechanisms of different types on security cooperative dialogue. China has placed great emphasis on defense consultations and security dialogues with countries concerned. By now, China has established consultation mechanisms on defense and security with 22 countries such as the United States, Russia, Japan, Australia, Britain and France. And China has also developed military ties for security with such neighboring countries as Pakistan, India, Mongolia, Thailand, Vietnam and the Philippines.

Fifth, promoting and participating in regional security cooperation. China, in 1997, participated in the ASEAN Regional Forum (ARF), the only official security and cooperation forum in the Asian-Pacific region. China hosted the first security policy meeting of the ARF in 2004, filling a gap in the dialogue of senior defense officers within the framework of ARF. In recent years, Chinese armed forces have participated in such dialogue mechanisms as the West Pacific Naval Forum and Shangri-la dialogue session, and carried out effective exchanges and co-operations in the fields of anti-terrorism, disaster relief, peacekeeping, maritime security and joint patrols in border areas.

Sixth, promote military transparency. China has issued White Paper on China's national defense every other year since 1995, and has issued six by 2009, introducing China's national defense policy and the status of China's defense and armed forces. Additionally, China has taken part in the UN's transparency

The Chinese navel fleet to Gulf of Aden and Somali under the escort mission in 2008.

system for military expenditures, and issued white papers on issues concerning security such as arms control and non-proliferation and space policy. Seventh, holding joint military exercises with other countries. In October 2002, China and Kyrgyzstan engaged in a joint anti-terrorism military exercise in their border area, which was China's first joint military exercise with foreign armed forces. By 2008, China has had 28 major joint military exercises with armed forces of countries concerned. In addition, China has invited foreign military delegations in China and observers of other countries to observe PLA's military drills, another major means of exchanges with foreign armed forces.

Seventh, hold joint military exercises with other countries. In October 2002, China and Kyrgyzstan took a joint anti-terrorism military exercise in their border area, which was China's first joint military exercise with foreign armed forces. In the ten years that followed, the People's Liberation Army has conducted 28 joint military exercise and 34 joint military drills with 31 countries in accordance with the agreements and arrangements reached between China and these respective countries. In addition, China has invited foreign military delegations in China and observers of other countries to observe PLA's military drills, another major means of exchanges with foreign armed forces.

Eighth, take full and active participation in international peacekeeping operations and international relief and rescue activities. Since the PLA dispatched its military observers to the UN's peacekeeping operations for the first time in 1990, China has sent more than 22,000 person-times of military personnel and police to 24 UN peacekeeping operations by 2013. Besides, China International Search and Rescue Team, composed mainly of Chinese servicemen, has since 2002 undertaken 36 urgent international humanitarian aid missions, and transported relief materials worth more than RMB 1.25 billion to 27 disaster-stricken countries provided more than a dozen disaster relief missions in emergencies to people stricken by the Indian Ocean tsunami, Katrina hurricane in US, South-Asian earthquakes and mudflow in the Philippines.

Ninth, participate in international convoys in the high seas. In line with the relevant resolutions of the United Nations Security Council (UNSC), and with the consent of the Transitional Federal Government of Somalia, the Chinese government dispatched a combined naval task force to conduct escort operations in the Gulf of Aden and waters off Somalia on December 26, 2008. As of December 2012, the Chinese Navy has dispatched, in 13 task groups, 34 warships, 28 helicopters, and 910 Special Operations Force (SOF) soldiers, escorting 4,984 ships in 532 batches.

China's military diplomacy has made contributions to the Chinese foreign-policy task of creating a favorable peripheral environment and building a harmonious world. Its status and function are becoming increasingly prominent as China develops.

Public Diplomacy

As economic globalization and information society develops, China's diplomacy has become a focus of public attention both home and abroad. Due to the differences in position and the angels of their perception, however, the domestic and international public has different views and interpretations on China's power, international stand, role, and foreign policy. To properly handle the relations between China's diplomacy and the general public and to win their understanding and support have become an imperative task for China's diplomacy. This section of diplomatic work is called public diplomacy, which is becoming brisk and dynamic.

In July 2009, the then Secretary General of CPC Central Committee Hu Jintao elaborated at the 11th Conference of Chinese Diplomatic Envoys Stationed Abroad, on the important status and role of public diplomacy. He pointed out that public diplomacy is not only an imperative for China to improve its diplomatic layout under the new situation, but also a new horizon for its diplomacy. He also emphasized the task of public diplomacy is to make to increase China's political influence, economic competitiveness, international appeal and moral support. The role of public diplomacy became prominent ever since.

Public diplomacy is a continuation and extension of traditional diplomacy. The Chinese official understanding of it is that public diplomacy "is usually led by the government, which uses various means of publicity and communications to present to foreign audiences its basic national conditions and policies, and to inform its own citizens of its foreign policy and related measures. The purpose is to win the understanding, recognition and support of the public both in the country and abroad, project a positive image of the country and the government, create a favorable media environment, and safeguard and advance the fundamental interests of the country in question."

The emphasis of public diplomacy in China indicates the changing perception of top Chinese leaders on this new form of diplomacy. The Chinese Foreign Ministry organized different public diplomacy activities coordinately when Chinese leaders visited foreign countries or attended multilateral conferences, such as arranging special interviews by the media, meeting the press jointly with foreign leaders, giving public lectures, having dinner parties with people from different professions and fields so that they can meet and communicate with broader range of the general public and have the opportunities to explain China's foreign policy principle and position from different perspective in a face-to-face manner in the countries they visited. Chinese leaders visiting foreign countries publish articles in the mainstream media during their visit and the Chinese diplomatic envoys stationed abroad do so elaborating China's policy on specific issue or in specific field in local media, airing the Chinese voice to enhance local public's understanding of China's diplomacy.

The press spokesperson system of the Chinese Foreign Ministry has been perfected: from only one press meeting without answering questions in a week

On December 31, 2012, China Public Diplomacy Association held the establishment meeting in Beijing. Li Zhaoxing, former Foreign Minister and member of the Foreign Affairs Committee of the NPC, was elected chairman of the association.

when it first started in 1983 to two press meetings per week to having news briefing every day. In the year of 2012, the Foreign Ministry held 200 press meetings and answered 3000 questions, which greatly facilitated the media to get information from the government. On important diplomatic occasion such as high level visits, the Foreign Ministry held special briefings to both Chinese and foreign media, introducing the background, goals of the visit and illuminate China's policy position so as to provide timely information about Chinese leaders' foreign tour or their participation of the conference. Such activities coordinated and facilitated foreign media in China and help them to have a comprehensive understanding and objective coverage of China.

The Chinese Foreign Ministry has established a special agency of public diplomacy and invited the director generals of the relevant departments to have direct online dialogue with Chinese netizens, organized on-line talks on "My View on Diplomacy", Lanting Forum and the Foreign Ministry's open day events to invite attentive public to visit the Foreign Ministry. Such activities provided new channels for all walks of life to discuss Chinese foreign policy and other foreign affairs topics of common interests. Such activities strengthened communication with the domestic media and general public so that the Foreign Ministry can solicit their opinions and benefit from their wisdom. In 2013, the Foreign Ministry promoted the formation of the China Public Diplomacy Association (CPDA) to muster social resources and garner non-governmental forces to promote the study on public diplomacy. CPDA also creates a platform by holding academic seminars to bridge the Chinese Foreign Ministry and high level government officials both home and abroad, academia, industrial and business circle, media and the general public.

Making use of modern technology and establishing Web Portal and bringing the government's Web Portal to play the role of the first platform of information transparency is another highlight of China's public diplomacy. In the year of 2012, the Ministry of Foreign Affair's web sites released more than 190,000 pieces of news and provided 80,000 news stories. China's 234 diplomatic missions abroad have all followed suite to start their web page as of 2013. In order to provide information about China's diplomacy, relevant departments of the Foreign Ministry have introduced such microblogs as "Sino-EU messenger (Department of Western European Affairs)," "Come to Africa (Department of Africa)", which have their micro-blog group and have effectively expanded their news coverage.

The Foreign Ministry and the State Council's Information Office have jointly published *China Diplomacy* white paper and Photo Album of China's Foreign Affairs annually elaborating China's diplomacy and China's position on international affairs. From 1991 when the State Council's Information Office published the first white paper on China's human right situation to 2013, it has published 88 white papers on different areas in cooperation with relevant ministries. These white papers intend to tell the world true stories of China and China's policy in different domains, enhancing international understanding of China.

The press spokesperson system of the Foreign Ministry has been universalized within the Chinese government. By 2013, 75 departments of the State Council, 31 provinces (autonomous regions and municipalities) and NPC, CPPCC, the Supreme Court, the Supreme People's Procuratorate and the 13 main departments of the CPC Central Committee have all established the press spokesperson system. The Ministry of Defense has institutionalized its spokesperson system since it was inaugurated in September 2007.

The Chinese Government considered public diplomacy an important vehicle for the development of soft power and has increased investment in public diplomacy from strategic perspective, including the increased investment in foreign languages communication and disseminating channels. Public diplomacy has become a new growth point and focus of China's diplomatic work. Its status and role in China's overall diplomacy is growing and its importance increasingly obvious.

Multilevel Foreign Relations

Summit diplomacy

Summit diplomacy refers to the diplomatic activities of the heads of the state or heads of government. Its traditional forms include such activities as visits by heads of state or government, summit meetings, correspondence and phone calls between heads of state or government, dispatching envoys or personal representatives abroad, or delivering foreign policy pronouncements in person.

On Oct. 1, 1949, Mao Zedong proclaimed in the *Notice of Central People's Government of the People's Republic of China* that "our government is the sole legal government representing the people of People's Republic of China. It is ready to establish diplomatic relations with all foreign governments that are willing to abide by the principles of equality, mutual benefit and mutual respect for each other's territorial integrity and sovereignty." This could be regarded as the first summit diplomacy with which New China's diplomacy started.

However, summit diplomacy was not quite active due to various reasons. New China's summit diplomacy during the Cold War was limited to only a few forms, including the issuance of statements and conversations, or paying visits to other countries by Chinese heads of state or government or receiving visits by their counterparts. During the 1950s and the 1960s, China's summit diplomacy was restricted to its relations with those countries in Asia, Africa, and Europe, which had diplomatic relations with China. For instance, as the chairman of both the Central People's Government and the Communist Party of China, Mao Zedong only made two foreign visits in his life and both were to the Soviet Union.

In February 1950, China and Soviet Union signed the Sino-Soviet Treaty of Friendship, Alliance and Mutual Assistance when Mao Zedong visited Soviet Union.

Since the 1980s, the rapid process of globalization has made summit diplomacy more prominent in international affairs due to these facts: The globalization of international challenges requires leaders from different countries to engage in direct discussions on measures to address them; the media in an age of information globalization has rendered summit diplomacy, especially the summit visits, to be the focuses or hotspots of the world; summit diplomacy could enable the supreme leaders of countries to engage in face-to-face negotiation so as to efficiently settle the problems they face.

The changes in international situations have led to proactive summit diplomacy in China. Hotlines have been frequently used for communications between Chinese heads of government and state with their counterparts. Bilateral and multi-lateral summit conferences have become highlights in the diplomatic arena. Envoy visits have become very popular diplomatic activities. Furthermore, the number of China's summit visits abroad has boomed, covering countries in Asia, Africa, Europe, Oceania, North America and Latin America. For instance, Jiang Zemin paid visits to more than 70 counties during his term in office from 1989 to 2002 as General Secretary of the CPC and as the president of PRC. In less than one year after they assumed Presidency and Premiership, Xi Jinping and Li Keqiang have made seven foreign trips visiting 22 countries in Europe, Asia, Africa and America. During the same period of time they received 60 plus visit of foreign head of state or head of government.

As the mode of diplomacy at the highest level, summit diplomacy has been the major way for China to settle important problems with related countries, and summits were usually landmark events in China's diplomatic history. At the end of 1949, soon after New China was founded, Chairman Mao Zedong paid a visit to the Soviet Union, and at the beginning of the next year, Premier Zhou Enlai also visited the Soviet Union. The visits by the heads of state and government of China immediately to the same country in the wake of the founding of the PRC

In May 1989, Deng Xiaoping met with Gorbachev, chairman of Presidium of the Supreme Soviet and General Secretary of the Communist Party of Soviet Union in Beijing.

by themselves were indications of New China's diplomatic strategy of "lean to one side." During this visit, China and the Soviet Union signed the *Sino-Soviet Treaty of Friendship, Alliance and Mutual Assistance*, which was of strategic significance for the PRC. Thirty years later, the normalization of Sino-Soviet relations was only realized after the meeting between Chinese leader Deng Xiaoping and Soviet leader Gorbachev, which "ends the past, and opens up the future" in bilateral relations. After the disintegration of the Soviet Union, summit diplomacy helped the bilateral relationship experience a successful transition from Sino-Soviet relations to Sino-Russian relations, making Sino-Russian relations institutionalized and experienced step by step. In less than one year after Xi became President, he has met Russian President on five different occasions, a testimony of the stable Sino-Russian relations.

Summit diplomacy also demonstrates the status of China's relations with different countries. Chinese leaders visited the United States only after the establishment of Sino-U.S. diplomatic relations. The exchanged visits of heads of state and government between China and the U.S. in the mid-1980s manifested the stable development of the bilateral relationship. To the contrary, after the U.S. president imposed sanctions against China in 1989, the exchange of visits at the highest level between the two countries was suspended for nine years. The frequent exchanges of visits by leaders of the two countries reveal the sound Sino-US relations today. For example, President Hu Jintao and President Bush had four meetings and four telephone conversations, and exchanged correspondences 10 times in 2008. In the less than five year before he became President, Xi Jinping had nine "talks" with American President Obama, including face-to-face meetings, conversations over telephone, exchange message, dispatching special envoys, etc. ensuring the smooth transition after the new administrations were formed in the two countries. During their meeting in Annenberg Estate, California in June 2013, they had 8 hours face to face conversation in two meetings in two days and had exchanged views extensively on bilateral relations. Summit diplomacy is not only the symbol of the stable

On February 19, 2014, President Xi Jinping and Pakistani President Hussein attended the signing ceremony of bilateral cooperation documents.

development of Sino-U.S. relations but also provides opportunities to enhance and advance Sino-U.S. relations, becoming the "ballast" of those relations.

And the same applies to the Sino-Japanese relationship. From 1979 to 1991, the Chinese heads of state and government made five visits to Japan. However, because of the mistaken stance by the Japanese leader at the beginning of the 21st century, China suspended the exchanged visits between the two countries, and then the bilateral relationship was trapped in a coexistence of "frosty diplomatic ties and hot economic ties." The exchanged visits were not resumed until the new leader of Japan changed the mistaken stance. Such visits as the "ice-breaking journey" by the Japanese premier Shinzo Abe to China in April 2006, the "ice-melting trip" by the Chinese premier Wen Jiabao to Japan in 2007, the "early spring journey" by the Japanese premier Yasuo Fukuda to China in December 2007, and the "warm spring journey" by the Chinese president Hu Jintao to Japan in May 2008, indicated that the Sino-Japanese relationship had returned to the right path, and were in the process of being promoted. Japan's "nationalization" of Chinese territory Diaoyu Islands deteriorated the bilateral relations. When high level exchange visit between China and most its neighbors happened frequently, Sino-Japanese summit diplomacy has been suspended so far. Such situation not only demonstrated the current status of Sino-Japanese relations, negatively impacted the bilateral relations but also hindered the regional integration process in East Asia.

Summit diplomacy has functioned as a significant driving force in bilateral relations. The most eye-catching summit visits or meetings are good examples. Each summit visit was accompanied by large political, economic, cultural, and other delegations, which would sign cooperation agreements with their counterparts during the summit visit in the fields of politics, security, trade and economy, energy, education, healthcare, culture, and tourism. The execution of these agreements would become the follow-up harvest of the summit visit, and become the major means to further promote and substantiate the bilateral cooperation. Furthermore, the interpersonal relations between the leaders established during these summit visits would become important links to cement bilateral relations, which will be conducive to developing long-term bilateral relations and enhancing mutual understanding.

Multilateral summit diplomacy has become the high-profile form of summit diplomacy nowadays epitomized by China's summit diplomacy. In order to settle such global problems as economic development and environment, China has participated in the global summits conferences held under the framework of UN. The extended G8 summit with leaders of leading developing countries, and the G20 summit conferences have been frequently held to cope with global problems of economy and economic crises, as well as other summit meetings with some regional and trans-regional multilateral organizations, such as Shanghai Cooperation Organization, ASEAN-China, East Asian Summit among Japan and South Korea, Asian and Pacific Economic Cooperation (APEC), and Asian-Europe Meeting (ASEM). As the leaders of the biggest developing country, China's heads of state and government have taken an active part in those multilateral summit conferences in which they elaborated China's view and put forward constructive proposals contributing China's wisdom to the settlement of the relevant problems under discussion.

Parliamentary diplomacy

Parliament is the legislative branch of a state, which occupies an important position in a country's social life and plays an important role in its politics. The external relations of the legislative body are an important component of the country's overall foreign relations, and are irreplaceable in enhancing mutual understanding and friendship with other peoples and pushing forward the development of diplomatic relations.

The National People's Congress (NPC) works as the legislative body of the People's Republic of China and the highest organ of state power in China. The foreign relations of the NPC and its standing committee have always played important roles in each phase of China's social evolution. After the reform and opening-up, as one important component of China's overall diplomacy, the relations of the NPC with the parliaments of developing countries in Asia, Africa, and Latin America have been deepened, and its relations with the parliaments of the Western countries have improved remarkably. Having become increasingly active in multilateral activities of parliament diplomacy, the foreign relations of the China's NPC have become omni-directional and multi-level, making it an important component of China's overall diplomacy.

The foreign relations of the China's NPC have made continuous advancements in recent years. First, the exchanges of visits between the Chinese NPC with its foreign counterparts at different levels have seen a gradual increase. For instance, chairman of the Standing Committee of the NPC, Wu Bangguo, had made 10 foreign visits, and members of the meeting of chairmen have made 58 foreign visits from 2003 to 2008, covering five continents. During the same time period, 109 speakers and vice speakers of foreign parliaments visited China upon being invited.

Second, China's NPC has established quite a few mechanisms of exchanges with foreign parliaments. From 1981, when the first exchange mechanism between NPC and the European Parliament was established, to 2013, the NPC has established exchange mechanism with more than 14 countries' parliaments and EU Parliament, including the U.S. House of Representatives and Senate, Russian Federal Committee and State Duma, Japan's Senate and Diet, South Korea's National Assembly, Indian parliament, the House of Representatives of Australia, Canadian parliament, British parliament, Germany's Bundestag, French Senate, the House of Representatives of Italy, South Africa's National Assembly, the People's Assembly of Egypt, and the House of Representatives of Brazil. In addition, the NPC has set up inter-parliamentary relations with

In June 2008, the Fifth Asia-Europe Parliamentary Partnership Meeting was held in Beijing.

178 countries, and founded 106 Friendship Groups under the framework of parliament with the principle of reciprocity, joined 15 multilateral parliamentary organizations and been an observer of 5 more such organizations.

Third, China's NPC has actively developed co-operations with and participated in multilateral affairs of the regional or global inter-parliamentary organizations. Up to 2013, China's NPC is the member of 12 international parliament organizations, such as World Conference of Speakers of Parliaments, Inter-Parliamentary Union, Asian Parliamentary Assembly, the Asian-Pacific Parliamentary Forum, Parlamento Latinoamericano, ASEAN Inter-Parliamentary Organization, Speakers Conference of Parliaments of Pacific Islands Forum, the Asia Europe Parliamentary Partnership Meeting and observer of three regional parliamentary organizations. China hosted the 12th annual meeting of the Asian-Pacific Parliamentary Forum in Beijing in 2004, and China's NPC hosted the fifth annual Asia-Europe Parliamentary Partnership Meeting in 2008.

The advantages and features of parliamentary diplomacy have been put to full use in China to push forward foreign exchanges, promote trade and economic co-operations, and to serve domestic construction. China's parliamentary diplomacy has achieved accomplishments and is playing a more and more important role in China's overall foreign relations.

Party diplomacy

The Communist Party of China is the leading party in China. The International Liaison Department of the CPC Central Committee is the functional department in charge of the foreign affairs of the Central Committee. As the leading party, the foreign relations of the CPC occupy an important role in China's comprehensive diplomacy and are an important part of China's overall foreign relations.

The goal of CPC's foreign relations or the goal of party diplomacy in China is to serve China's comprehensive diplomacy. In accordance with the special

need of the Party at different time periods, the adjustment of state's diplomatic task and the development in international situation, the target and forms of CPC's foreign relations have undergone changed during its history. When it was first funded, the CPC was a branch of the Intercom. From the founding of the PRC to the beginning of the 1960s, its targets were limited to the communist parties in socialist countries, labor party, communist parties in non-socialist countries and other progressive parties.

Having drawn experiences and lessons from the history of the party's foreign relations, the 12th CPC National Congress in 1982 began to plan its foreign relations within the overall China's foreign relations, while separating party-to-party relations from those inter-state relations, and put forward the principles of "independence, complete equality, mutual respect, and noninterference in each other's internal affairs" in developing relations with foreign parties. Thereafter the CPC has been willing to establish contact,

In April 2013, the fourth China-Europe High-Level Political Parties Forum was convened in Suzhou, Jiangsu Province.

communication and cooperation of different kind with any parties that are willing to communicate with CPC, expanding from communist parties in different countries and other left-wing parties to nationalist and democratic parties in the majority of developing countries, social parties, labor parties, conservative parties as well as parties, statesman, and international organizations with different ideology and nature in developed countries. CPC maintains extensive exchanges and cooperation with 600 parties in 160 countries and other political organizations including ruling parties, coalition parties, lawful opposition parties, regional organizations of parties and regional parties.

During this process, the tasks of the CPC foreign relations of have also undergone changes from enhancing relations with communist parties and labor parties in order to gain international support and assistance, which were badly needed at that time, in the early days after the PRC's founding to multi-level exchanges after China's opening-up. Today the content of the CPC's relations with other foreign parties cover a broad domain, both consultations on new ways to improve interstate relations and exploring new means for party building; both political dialogue and economic and cultural exchanges; both visits and investigations and theoretical exploration; both exchanges idea on policies to run state and administrate government and bring stability and prosperity to the country and seeking solutions to regional and international problems. Party diplomacy has become an important channel to promote the development of China's foreign relations.

Different political forces in the world underwent reshuffles and realignments after the end of the Cold War, and parties with different political stances and thoughts are becoming ever more active. In conformity with the changes and development in the international situation, the CPC has established relations with more foreign parties, with the level of exchanges increased, the content of exchanges substantiated, and areas of the exchanges expanded, forming a framework of all-round, multi-channel, extensive and in-depth

Additionally, the CPC has also taken an active part in multilateral activities of international parties. Having participated in the first and second International Conference of Asian Political Parties, the CPC hosted in Beijing in 2008 the third International Conference of Asian Political Parties, which was attended by leaders and delegates of 81 political parties from 35 countries. The conference has greatly enhanced the mutual understanding between the CPC and other political parties from other Asian countries in the new era.

The foreign relations of the CPC have consolidated and enhanced the relationship between the CPC and the ruling parties of socialist countries, enriched the forms and substances with the political parties in developing countries, strengthened the relations with major parties in developed countries, and promoted mutual understanding with the parties of those countries that have not established diplomatic relations with China, facilitating a favorable condition for the final normalization of diplomatic ties between China and these countries.

Enhance mutual understanding by civil diplomacy

Civil diplomacy is the conduct of international relations in civil terms, which is different from the diplomacy by government. Put it plainly, civil diplomacy is the diplomacy of making friends, which is also referred to as people-to-people diplomacy. It focuses on enhancing trust and understanding between peoples, attaches great importance to communications, and emphasizes establishing friendships that go beyond concrete political and economic interests. Civil diplomacy has been an important channel to enhance mutual contacts and understanding between countries and its importance has become prominent against the background of globalization.

China has always put a great emphasis on civil diplomacy, and has put forward the ideas of "relying on the people and placing hope on them" in diplomatic practice. In order to enhance the mutual understanding between China and the outside world, the Chinese People's Congress of Defending World Peace, which was merged with the Chinese People's Association for Friendship with Foreign Countries in 1972, and Chinese People's Institute of Foreign Affairs were created in the wake of the founding of New China. China Council for the Promotion of International Trade was founded in 1952 to promote China's trade and economic co-operations with foreign countries. In 1954, these organizations joined hands with more than 10 other non-governmental organizations, including All China Federation of Trade Unions and All China Women's Federation, to form the Chinese People's Association for Foreign Culture, which was renamed the Chinese People's Association for Friendship with Foreign Countries in 1969 to enhance friendships with foreign people, promote international cooperation, maintain world peace, and make friends on the international stage. The tradition of civil diplomacy in China has taken shape.

Under the special international environment after the foundation of New China, civil diplomacy has enhanced mutual understandings between the Chinese people and Japanese people and improved Sino-Japanese relationship by means of "economic ties promoting political ties, and civil ties promoting official ties." Civil diplomacy, which has played an indispensable role in facilitating the normalization of Sino-Japanese diplomatic ties, occupies an important position in the history of China's foreign relations.

Since China's reform and opening-up, especially in the 21st century, the Chinese People's Association for Friendship with Foreign Countries, the main institution of civil diplomacy in China, has coordinated the overall situation both home and abroad and set the following guidelines in developing civil diplomacy: Create civil cooperative relations with great powers, including U.S., Russia, Japan, and European Union (group of powers). Make these relations, and the relations with China's neighbors, a priority. Civil relations with developing countries are the focus. Multilateral civil diplomacy with international non-governmental organizations is new areas to be expanded. Make efforts to develop civil relations with countries that have not established diplomatic relations

2012 China International Friendship Cities Conference was held in Chengdu, Sichuan Province in September 2012.

with China in order to facilitate the diplomatic goal of creating a favorable international and peripheral environment for China's domestic construction of economy. For instance, when Sino-Japanese relations were trapped in a deadlock at the turn of the 21st century, the Chinese People's Association for Friendship with Foreign Countries and 17 other friendship groups from both China and Japan gathered in Beijing in 2001 to issue the *Declaration of Sino-Japanese Civil Friendship in the New Century*. In 2005, the Chinese People's Association for Friendship with Foreign Countries hosted another gathering in Tokyo, Japan with participation from 60 friendship groups from the two countries and issued the *Appeal for Peace and Good-neighborly Friendship*. The civil diplomacy between China and Japan helped maintain the stability of the bilateral relations, even as exchanges of official visits at the highest level were suspended between the two countries.

The activities between international friendship cities have been another major channel and important form of civil diplomacy. With the development of China's modernization, urbanization in China has been booming. The foreign relations of Chinese cities and other local governments with their foreign counterparts have become important channels for China's integration with the international community and an important link with the outside. Since the first sister cities between Tianjin, China and Kobe, Japan in 1973, thirty provinces, autonomous regions and municipalities in China (excluding Taiwan Province, Hong Kong and Macau Special Administrative Region) and 433 cities have established 2083 sister city (province or state) with 463 provinces (state, county, region, circuit) and 1423 cities in five continents by the end of 2013.

In 1992, the Chinese People's Association for Friendship with Foreign Countries created the China International Friendship Cities Association, which joined the International Union of Local Authorities in 1999. China has hosted the 2008, 2010 and 2012 International Sister City Conference. The inter-city cooperation is growing from bilateral form to multilateral form, and is gradually moving from people-to-people cooperation to covering all the fields, including politics, economy, culture, and society. It has contributed to enhancing China's exchanges and cooperation with the world in such fields as economy, culture, education, science and technology, and urban construction.

Promoting bilateral friendships by setting up bilateral friendship associations is another important form of China's civil diplomacy. In October 1949, China set up the first bilateral friendship association, All China Congress of Sino-Soviet Friendship Association (renamed Sino-Russian Friendship Association in 1992). For civil friendships to Japan, the Sino-Japanese Friendship Association was founded in 1963. Both of them played important roles in promoting the Sino-Soviet relationship (Russian) and the Sino-Japanese relationship. Up until 2013, China had established 46 inter-regional or transnational friendship associations, including China-E.U. Friendship Association, China-Arabian Countries Friendship Association, China-ASEAN Friendship Association, China-Central Asia Friendship Association, and China-U.S. Friendship Association. In addition, China had established friendly cooperation with 500 NGOs in 157

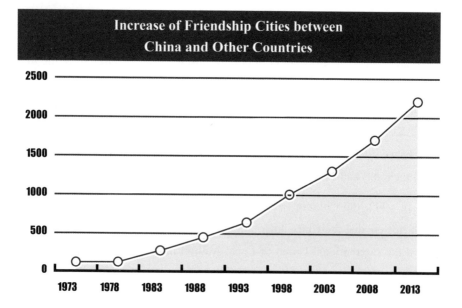

Increase of Friendship Cities between
China and Other Countries

countries. By developing none-official exchanges, organizing exchanges of visit, initiating and host seminar, talks, forum and other activities of exchanges, non-official diplomacy help establish communication mechanism, form cooperative platforms, and enhance mutual understanding between peoples and build up trust and development friendship.

Having played an irreplaceable role in the diplomatic history of the PRC, civil diplomacy continues to enhance the friendship between the Chinese people and the peoples around the world, promoting China's economic and cultural exchanges and co-operations with foreign countries. It has become another manifestation of China's integration into the world.

Globalization has posed unprecedented challenges for contemporary diplomacy. While coping with these challenges, China has found opportunities therein and has put forward the notion of "comprehensive diplomacy" to call attention to the overall situation while managing foreign affairs. Its core purpose is still to create a favorable international environment for China's domestic economic construction, to maintain world peace, to promote common development, and to build a harmonious world of peace and prosperity.

Conclusion

The PRC is 64 years old and China's diplomacy also has gone through a journey of 64 years.

The 64-year history of the PRC can be divided into the first 30 years after its founding and the second 34 years since its opening-up and reform in 1978. The major diplomatic task of the first 30 years was to oppose the threat from big powers, consolidate national independence, and safeguard sovereignty and territorial integrity. The second 30 years was dedicated to creating a good international and peripheral environment for its domestic economic construction and to promote China's development in accordance with the development and changes of the international situation.

The two 30-year periods of China's diplomatic history have remarkably different features of their respective times and are intimately related to each other. The first 30 years scored great achievements in consolidating the state and safeguarding independence. More specifically, the New China had a clear break with the old diplomacy of humiliation; stabilized the new kind of diplomatic relations with other countries on the basis of equality and mutual benefit; secured equal position and dignity on the global stage; gained diplomatic independence by safeguarding and strengthening state independence, and protected national security and territorial integrity; settled the boundary disputes left over from history with most neighbors through peaceful means, and created a stable neighborhood in general improving relations with neighbors; established strong friendship with the vast majority of developing countries through mutual support; set up a new type of diplomatic force, providing the personnel guarantee for the diplomacy of independence.

The third session of the 11th plenary of the The Communist Party of China's Central Committee ushered in a new epoch in Chinese history and landed China's diplomacy into a new era. Holding high the banner of peace and development, China's diplomacy since then has inherited the past and scored the new achievements.

First of all, China's diplomacy has created a peaceful international and peripheral environment for domestic economic development by ensuring the sustained and stable high economic growth rate domestically, and by raising China's comprehensive national strength and its international competitiveness. China's gross domestic product (GDP) has increased from RMB 364.5 billion in 1978 to more than RMB 56.8845 trillion in 2013. China's contribution to world economic growth has surpassed more than 10 percent, and China's national power today is incomparable with that in the past.

Second, China has been actively integrated into the international community, forming a benign interaction with the outside world. China has joined more than 100 inter-governmental international organizations, acceded more than 300 international multilateral treaties, participated in 24 UN peace-keeping operations, and dispatched more than 22,000 peacekeeping personnel. All of this makes China an important actor in the international world. While integrating into the international economic system, China, in conformity with the trends of economic globalization, has actively participated in the activities of the international community, and insisted on its identity as a developing country to make its utmost effort to enhance and promote the interests of developing countries according to the principle of balancing between rights and obligations. At the same time, China has coordinated and cooperated efficiently with different international institutions, making the country better adapt to the international community.

Third, China upholds justice in international affairs and has become a responsible power with its status on the international stage gradually upgraded. China stands for peaceful negotiation and diplomatic consultation in the settlement of global and regional conflicts, assumes due international responsibilities, and lives up to its commitments in the settlement of such global issues as global climate change and public health. China's proactive policies have been fully recognized by the international community. China's contributions to world peace and development in the last 30 years are greater than any time in its history, and China's international image is better than ever before.

Fourth, China's diplomatic front has been gradually extended with a good foreign relations structure of omni-direction. Currently China maintains diplomatic relations with 171 countries. In its relations with developed countries, China holds the principle of surpassing the differences in social systems and ideologies in order to develop relations with them, seeking common ground while reserving differences. China adheres to dialogue while avoiding confrontation, properly manages differences and frictions, expands the areas where the two sides' interests meet, and establishes strategic partnerships of various types and cooperative relations with different countries, creating a sound situation of overall development of diplomatic relations. In conformity with the principle of equal consultation, mutual understanding and mutual accommodation, China has signed boundary agreements or treaties with 12 of its 14 land neighbors and solved 90 percent of its land border disputes or has reached provincial agreements on those that are still difficult to solve according to the principle of "shelving the disputes," creating a peaceful, stable, cooperative and win-win peripheral environment on the basis of equality and mutual trust—making its relations with its neighbors the best in the annals of history. In relations with other developing countries, China has emphasized its commitment to continue to enhance the solidarity and cooperation with them. In addition to providing assistance to some of them to the best of China's capability, China has increasingly expanded the areas of cooperation, explored new ways to cooperate, increased the efficiency of cooperation with them according to the principle of "equality and mutual benefit, emphasizing practical results, diversity in forms, and attainment of common development."

Given the new domestic and international situation, China has endeavored to coordinate domestic development and opening-up, and has advocated the concept of comprehensive diplomacy of promoting security diplomacy, economic diplomacy, and humanitarian diplomacy. China has developed economic cooperation with all countries, promoted dialogues and communications with other civilizations, and increased the knowledge about and understanding of China by the international community.

Through 60 plus years of thick and thin, China's diplomacy has accumulated a wealth of experience. China has realized that China cannot develop without the world and the world cannot become prosperous without China. The future and fate of China has been intimately tied with the rest of the world. Whatever changes take place in the international situation, China promises that: the Chinese government and people will always hold high the banner of peace, development and cooperation, pursue an independent foreign policy of peace, safeguard China's interests in terms of sovereignty, security and development, and uphold its foreign policy purposes of maintaining world peace and promoting common development.

The Chinese government and people will continue to contribute to regional and global development through its own development, and expand the areas where China's interests meet with those of various sides. While securing its own development, China will accommodate the legitimate concerns of other countries, especially other developing countries. The Chinese government and people will increase market access in accordance with internationally recognized economic and trade rules, and protect the rights and interests of our partners in accordance with relevant laws. China will continue to support international efforts to help developing countries enhance their capacity for independent development and improve the lives of their people so as to narrow the North-South gap. The Chinese government and people will continue to support the efforts to improve international trade and financial systems, advance the liberalization and facilitation of trade and investment, and properly resolve economic and trade frictions through consultation and collaboration.

Reviewing China's 60-plus-year journey, we see China's diplomacy has come to a new height. Looking into the future, we believe that China's diplomacy is at a new starting point. As China becomes stronger with an upgraded status on the international stage, China's diplomacy is facing greater missions, and the burden is heavy and the road is long. What can be trusted is that China will adhere to the road of peaceful development and that the Chinese people will join the peoples from all other countries to make dedicated efforts to realize the beautiful desires of human beings.

Recall the past 60 plus years, earth-shaking changes have taken place in both China's domestic and international environment. China's national power today is in a position that the past cannot be compared, its status on the world stage has been much elevated, and the Chinese people's living standard has been improved remarkably. China's contribution to the world is on the rise and a virtuous circle has been formed in the inaction between China and the world. China's diplomacy has played an indispensable role during the process when these achievements were accomplished.

Look into the future, China's diplomacy is standing at a new height with a new starting point. Today China's diplomacy enjoys a larger platform with bigger responsibilities. It attracts more attention and holds higher expectations. To realize the Chinese dream of great national rejuvenation, China needs world peace and a sound international environment. The burden of China's diplomacy is heavy and the road is long. It is entrusted with a major mission and has bright prospects.